NEW RECIPES FROM YC

SANDWICH MAKER

Revised Edition

DONNA RATHMELL GERMAN

Bristol Publishing Enterprises
Hayward, California

A **nitty gritty**® Cookbook

Printed in the United States of America.

ISBN: 1-55867-285-0

Cover design: Frank J. Paredes
Cover photography: John A. Benson
Food stylist: Susan Broussard
Illustrator: James Balkovek

CONTENTS

Sing a song of sandwich, a pocket made with rye;

Lots of meats and cheeses baked in a pie.

When the machine was opened, the kids began to sing:

Isn't that a dainty dish to set before the king?

This book is dedicated to my three kitchen helpers,

Rachel, Katie and Helen; and to their father, Lee.

ABOUT SANDWICH MAKERS AND SANDWICHES

Your sandwich maker is a convenience appliance which adapts easily to your busy lifestyle. Most people these days are on the run all the time. Hot food from a sandwich maker is quick and easy, and especially convenient when you only want to make enough food for one or two. The result is easy to carry and easy to eat. In addition, the sandwich maker is a handy tool for the host or hostess who wants to spend time with guests rather than in food preparation.

The sandwich maker opens up a whole new world of fast, simple cooking — hot sandwiches, of course, but many other foods: omelets, French toast, pancakes, muffins, quick breads, cakes and even pies. In addition to bread, you can fill wrappers such as tortillas, puff pastry, crescent roll dough and pizza dough. Your sandwich maker can make breakfast fare, delicious small appetizers, entrées such as enchiladas and egg rolls, and scrumptious desserts.

This book provides recipes, directions and ideas for all of these items and more. There are no firm rights or wrongs in sandwich making as long as you are happy with the results. Use the recipes in this book as guides in sandwich making, but use your imagination to create other winning combinations. Note that many of the recipes in this book assume that your sandwich maker shapes your sandwiches so that they are sealed around the edges, allowing you to have wet fillings. Some sandwich makers — or panini makers — do not shape sandwich edges in this way. Use common sense in making and adapting your recipes to your own sandwich maker.

We have come a long way from the 4th Earl of Sandwich, John Montagu (1718-1792) who, not wanting to leave the gaming table, asked for his meat between two slices of bread so that he could continue to play. The Earl of Sandwich had no idea that he was creating not only a new dish, but an entirely new lifestyle of eating, and that his name would eventually be linked to a unique way of convenient food preparation: the popular sandwich maker.

GENERAL DIRECTIONS FOR SANDWICH MAKERS

DIRECTIONS FOR A REGULAR SANDWICH

Some recipes require all or part of the filling ingredients to be mixed together and spread on the inside of the bread or wrapper. Other recipes simply require layering the ingredients and placing them on the inside of the bread, leaving a 1/4-inch border. Close the sandwich, coat the outside of the bread with margarine, butter, vegetable or olive oil if desired and heat for about 2 to 4 minutes until done to taste. Watch the sandwich to avoid burning. After the first 1 1/2 minutes of cooking, it is okay to lift the lid to see if the sandwich looks done. If using a wrapper such as tortillas, pizza dough or puff pastry, please see *Ingredients*, pages 4–7, for cooking guidelines.

If substituting slices of meat or cheese in place of diced or grated, always make sure that you trim them to fit the bread and the machine, leaving a $1/4$-inch border of wrapper.

MACHINE HEAT SETTINGS

For the sake of consistency, all recipes were tested on medium heat settings on those machines which have settings. If your machine has different settings, feel free to experiment with them.

INGREDIENT AMOUNTS

Ranges are given for amounts of each ingredient (for example, $1-1\frac{1}{2}$ tsp., $1-2$ slices) to take into account varying thicknesses of meat cuts, thickness of bread slices and the capacity of your machine (which may hold from 3 tbs. to $5\frac{1}{2}$ tablespoons of filling). The ranges should give you a feel for the proportions I recommend, but your taste is ultimately the deciding factor.

MANUFACTURER'S DIRECTIONS

Your machine will last longer and give you the best results if used, maintained and cleaned according to the manufacturer's recommendations. Especially follow manufacturer's directions for use of aerosol sprays (some recommend against it) and preparing the scallops to make sandwiches without applying spreads or oils to the outside of the wrapper. There are differences in the surface coatings from machine to machine and they must, therefore, be treated differently.

SANDWICH INGREDIENTS

WRAPPERS

Wrappers for sandwiches, appetizers, entrées and desserts do not have to be limited to breads. Vary the wrappers that you use and, if using breads, vary the bread for new and delicious sandwiches.

While you may trim your wrapper to fit the machine, sometimes it is easier to trim the sandwich after it has cooked. That may cut down on overflows.

Descriptions of wrappers (other than breads), of test results using those wrappers in the sandwich maker, and rankings of 1–5 (5 being the best) are provided here for comparison. The rankings are based on my opinion only. Your results may, of course, vary due to the particular ingredient used, the machine itself, and factors such as climate or altitude.

crescent roll dough, refrigerator biscuit dough — I refer here to dough purchased in tubes in the refrigerated section of your grocery store. The crescent roll dough forms a long rectangle which is divided into triangles. If you take one rectangular section and press the triangular seams together to seal, roll slightly with a rolling pin and cut in half, this should fit your machine perfectly. Likewise, refrigerator biscuit dough may be seamed together and rolled to fit the scallops. When using one of these as a wrapper, you need to use more filling to achieve a nice, full sandwich. Underfilling will result in the top not cooking properly. Heat the sandwich in the machine for about

2 to 3½ minutes. Results were not always consistent. When it worked well, this method produced beautiful, puffy sandwiches. Sometimes, however, the bottom piece would be too brown by the time the upper piece was cooked. Overall ranking: 3.

tortillas, egg roll wrappers, crepes and phyllo — Use a much larger amount of filling to compensate for the lack of thickness. I have found that it works better to cut (if necessary) these wrappers larger than the scalloped sections of the machine. Excess may always be trimmed after cooking; however, if there is too little wrapper, the edges won't seal properly. The area where the scallops seal the sandwich was often too brown before the sandwich was done. It is difficult to obtain picture-perfect results, but the taste is great. The one recipe which works absolutely wonderfully with tortillas is the Enchilada recipe, as the tortillas are dipped in sauce before cooking.

Thaw frozen phyllo according to package directions. Bake phyllo sandwiches for about 2 to 3 minutes. I preferred (other testers' opinions differ) a basic white bread or pizza dough to tortillas or phyllo. Overall rankings: tortillas 2–3; egg roll wrappers 1–2; crepes 1–2; phyllo 1

pie crust or puff pastry — Refrigerated unbaked pie crust I felt worked best. The puff pastry (sheets, not shells) should be thawed according to package directions. Once again, you need enough filling so that the upper piece of the dough is in direct contact with the upper scallop of the machine. You must latch the machine for the first minute or two and then unlatch it so that the dough may rise. Results varied from terrific to crumbly but with a great taste. Cook your sandwich for about 3 to 5 minutes. Overall ranking: 3–4.

pizza dough, frozen bread dough (either homemade or from a grocery store's refrigerated or frozen food section) — If using frozen dough, thaw according to package directions. Roll out and cut dough into squares to fit the machine. One word of caution: do not roll this dough too thinly. Cook sandwiches for about 3 to 4 minutes or until golden. This, of all the alternatives, is the one which I found to work the best. The resulting sandwiches took on the scalloped shapes nicely and had the flavor of just-baked bread. Overall ranking: 5.

MAKING PIZZA DOUGH FROM SCRATCH:

2–2½ tsp. yeast, or 1 pkg.

1⅓ cups lukewarm water (115º)

1 tbs. olive oil

¾ tsp. salt

4 cups bread flour or all-purpose flour, or 2 cups wheat flour and 2 cups bread flour

In a large bowl, sprinkle yeast over warm water and let sit in a warm, draft-free spot for 5 to 10 minutes. To this mixture gradually add olive oil, flour and salt, beating until smooth. Knead dough for about 10 minutes. Place dough in a large, greased bowl, cover with a kitchen towel and place on the top rack of a cold oven. On the bottom rack, place a 9 x 13-inch pan full of hot water. Let rise for 45 to 60 minutes. At this point, the dough may be placed in a plastic bag in the refrigerator for up to 3 days.

Roll out dough with a rolling pin and cut with a knife or pizza wheel to fit your machine. If using a bread machine, make the recipe on your dough cycle. The recipe may be cut in half for machines that make 1 lb. loaves (2 cups of flour). Please note that you may need to stop or unplug the machine after the first kneading and rising to prevent a second kneading. Of course, there is no harm in letting it knead a second time, it just takes longer!

MAKING YOUR OWN BREAD

Bread machines and frozen dough have now made fresh, hot, homemade bread available to every household with minimal effort. If you are the owner of a bread machine, I'm sure you are already enjoying the countless varieties of breads you can make. (If not, please look for my books, including *The Bread Machine Cookbook* and *The Bread Machine Cookbook II*.)

For variety, ingredients may be added to the dough to change the flavor and texture from a basic white loaf. Simply knead into it either at the end of the first kneading or during the second kneading 1 to 2 tbs. of any of the following ingredients:

fresh or dried oregano

fresh or dried basil

fresh or dried mint

coarsely ground black pepper

chopped nuts – walnuts, almonds, pecans, macadamias

grated cheeses – cheddar, Swiss or Parmesan

FILLINGS AND SPREADS

One of the main purposes of this book is to help provide recipes and ideas for your sandwich maker. Please do not feel limited to use only the ingredients in these recipes, but vary them to please yourself. Leave out an ingredient you don't like, or add one that is more to your taste. Here are some tips about ingredients.

Buy chunk cheeses and grate them all at once. Store them in resealable bags or airtight containers in the refrigerator. You may also buy pre-grated cheeses if desired.

Dice or chop vegetables all at once and store them in airtight containers in the refrigerator.

Cook large amounts of ground meat or bacon. Freeze in small amounts in airtight plastic containers or freezer bags so you can thaw and use only what you need.

Spices can add zest to any sandwich or meal. If you want to experiment with a new seasoning, taste a small amount alone or mix it into some cream cheese, cottage cheese or eggs to get an idea of the flavor. Don't overlook some of the spice blends or salt-free seasoning blends.

Don't be afraid to try new condiments on your sandwiches. On your next trip to the grocery store, take a moment to look at all the different kinds of mustards. Just using a new mustard provides a brand new taste. Explore chutneys, relishes, horseradish sauces and other condiments as well.

A cautionary note: there are a few foods which are wonderful in cold sandwiches but do not heat well, such as lettuce, which gets soggy, and avocado, which becomes bitter.

Don't forget leftovers, which can taste wonderful in sandwiches.

Outside spreads may consist of softened or melted margarine or butter, vegetable oil or olive oil. They may be used plain or seasoned with herbs or spices. If a sandwich calls for basil or oregano in the filling, dress the outside up with the same seasoning in your oil. Keep small containers of seasoned oil for up to 2 weeks. Measure a small amount of oil, perhaps 1/4–1/3 cup, and mix in your herbs (about 1 tsp.). All you need to do is brush the oil on the wrapper. If you use an outside oil or spread, your sandwich will be more golden. If no specific listing is made for an outside spread in the recipes that follow, you may use butter or vegetable oil.

To spice up your favorite combinations such as ham or chicken and cheese, try soaking the bread in an egg mixture and French toasting: see page 18 for the *Basic French Toast* recipe.

QUESTIONS AND ANSWERS

My sandwiches cook nicely but are pale in color. Why?

Bread will color little on its own. If you wish to have a beautifully golden sandwich, try using butter or oil on the outside of the bread. Experiment with butter, margarine or vegetable oil.

I occasionally use thinly sliced bread. Do I have to adjust recipes for that?

Yes. Ingredient amounts are given in a range. If using a thin bread or wrapper such as tortillas, you will require more filling to sufficiently toast the bread. Use the upper end of the given range or even more.

I am on a diet but the directions with my machine say to use butter on the outside of the bread. What should I do?

Using butter, margarine or oil on the outside of your bread will give a golden, toasted appearance along with the calories. It is not necessary to use anything on the outside of your wrapper, however. Your machine will probably need to be seasoned with a little vegetable oil to prevent sticking. This should be done every five to six times you use the machine. Check your owner's manual for specific directions related to your particular machine. Some manufacturers recommend against using an aerosol nonstick spray while others suggest it as an alternative to butter.

What should I do when my sandwiches stick and are difficult to remove?

Your machine may require seasoning with a vegetable oil. Consult your owner's manual for the best method to use for your machine.

Ingredients often spill out of the machine, making a mess. What should I do?

There could be two reasons for this:

1. Too much filling is being used; cut back proportionally.

2. Not enough border is being left on the wrapper. Make sure to leave enough room at the edges of the wrapper so that it will seal properly. I suggest at least $1/4$ inch.

The machine is sometimes very difficult to clean. I don't want to use an abrasive as it could hurt the finish. What should I do?

Cleaning the machines can be difficult sometimes. What I have found to work is a soft toothbrush for those hard-to-reach corners. Follow manufacturer's directions for general cleaning guidelines as some manufacturers recommend against using even a wet cloth. Not only is it difficult to clean the inside, but if ingredients spill to the outside, that can also be difficult to clean. As that is not the coated baking area, I have used cleansers; but, again, manufacturer directions should be checked.

When removed from the machine, the bread is cut by the scalloped edges, but the meat is not, causing the sandwich to fall apart or the meat to come out. How can I correct this?

Trim the sandwich after cooking along the perforations with a sharp knife. You could also dice the meat prior to inserting it into the sandwich. Diced meat makes the sandwich easier to eat as well.

What do you mean by a pinch or a dash?

A dash and a pinch are each equal to about $1/16$ teaspoon.

Can I make things like cookies and cakes in my sandwich maker?

Cakes, quick breads, and muffins cook nicely in the sandwich maker. See pages 152, 33 and 32 for directions. I have not had very good luck with cookies and therefore do not recommend them.

PARTY IDEAS AND MENUS

If you enjoy easy, no-fuss entertaining, your sandwich maker can be center stage. It's a great icebreaker, too, for those get-togethers where not all the guests know each other.

When you use your sandwich maker for parties, the preparation is easy — lay out fillings, side dishes such as salad or fruit, and beverages. No more standing over a hot stove as the guests are arriving. No matter what the time of day or age of the guests, your sandwich maker will make your party a better one.

What could be better or easier than setting out a selection of foods for a party for teenagers? They can make their own sandwiches or entrées just the way they want them. Younger children enjoy being able to pick out what they want and then put ingredients into the sandwich maker (with adult supervision of course). Breakfast or brunch, cocktail hour or buffet table are all perfect for this handy appliance!

The following menu ideas should spark your imagination.

PIZZA PARTY — GO ITALIAN

Italian favorites make a winning party combination for any age group. A cool, light dessert is the perfect finale.

Caesar salad
Italian sandwiches:
Pizza Sandwich, page 98
Calzone, page 99
Italian Sausage and Peppers sandwich, page
   100

Meatball Sandwich, page 101
Lazy Lasagna, page 102
Italian Sub, page 93
assorted sherbets

A LA MEXICANA — OLE

You can feed them well at a get-together with a Mexican theme. If you use tortillas for wrappers, trim them ahead of time for your guests.

Tossed green salad
Quesadillas, page 63
Cheesy Taco Appetizers, page 56

Quick and Easy Nachos, page 57
Enchiladas, page 122
assorted melon slices

ISLAND HOPPING

When you feel like you want to get away from it all, plan an island buffet and let everyone do his or her own thing.

fresh vegetable platter with yogurt dip
Macadamia and Cheeses, page 53
Pineapple Chicken, page 94
Coconut Shrimp, page 112
Hawaiian Ham, page 117

Macadamia Coconut Cheese Puffs, page 61
Peanut Chicken Tidbits, page 60
Brazilian Shrimp Empadinhas, page 127
fruit juice punch

ORIENTAL FLAVORS

Delicious Oriental favorites are easy to make with the sandwich maker. Add a salad and rice, and you have a meal.

won ton soup
Egg Roll, page 136
Lumpia, page 137
Peanut Chicken Tidbits, page 60

Oriental Chicken and Ham, page 106
Chinese tea
rice
assorted sauces (mustard, plum sauce, etc.)

SUPER BOWL SUNDAY (OR ANY FOOTBALL SUNDAY)

Put out assorted breads, meats, cheeses, condiments and seasonings, and let them make their own sandwiches at halftime.

assorted cold beers and soft drinks
Easy Combos, page 75

coleslaw
chips

SUNDAY BRUNCH

The easy way to have your friends over for a get-together. Arrange cheese, meats and vegetables in small bowls, beat the eggs and serve in a large bowl with a ladle. Let your guests tailor-make their own omelets.

coffee and tea
fruit compote

About Omelets, pages 34–37
toast, butter and assorted jams

BREAKFAST AND BRUNCH

You will find many favorite breakfast and brunch selections are uniquely suited to your sandwich maker — omelets, French toast, pancakes, muffins and quick breads all become quick work, and give you the added plus of allowing small, individual servings.

Most of the recipes in this section are provided on a per sandwich basis or individual serving, but are easily increased to fit your needs. A few are provided for multiple servings and are noted as such.

BASIC FRENCH TOAST

Some people, children especially, prefer the basics. And, yes, it can be done in the sandwich maker. You may want to slice the bread twice as thick as usual.

Bread: nut, raisin, white or whole wheat

	Single	Multiple
egg, beaten	1	3–4
milk or cream	2–3 tbs.	$1/3$–$1/2$ cup
cinnamon and/or nutmeg	to taste	to taste

Beat ingredients together and place in a bowl which is about the same size as your bread. The real trick to perfect French toast is the soaking — let the bread sit in the mixture for a minute or two instead of just dipping it in. For best results in the sandwich maker, soak only one side of each slice of bread in the egg mixture. Cook in your sandwich maker for about 3 minutes or until golden. Cinnamon or nutmeg may be sprinkled on the bread prior to cooking.

FRENCH TOAST WITH PRESERVES

What a variation on plain French toast! Serve with or without syrup depending on your sweet tooth.

Bread: nut, raisin, white or whole wheat

Egg Mixture: *Basic French Toast*, page 18

Filling

2–3 tbs. cream cheese
1–1½ tbs. favorite preserves
confectioners' sugar for garnish, optional

Mix filling ingredients together while bread is soaking in egg mixture. Spread filling on unsoaked side of bread, top with a second slice of soaked bread, and cook 2 to 4 minutes. Garnish with confectioners' sugar if desired.

BANANA FRENCH TOAST

Replace preserves with 4 to 5 slices of banana and sprinkle with chopped nuts if desired.

FRUITED FRENCH TOAST

A truly decadent way to start your day! You can substitute cottage cheese for the cream cheese.

Bread: white, nut, raisin or cinnamon

Egg Mixture: *Basic French Toast*, page 18

Filling

$1\frac{1}{2}$–2 tbs. cream cheese, softened

$1\frac{1}{2}$–2 tbs. fruit, diced, sliced or chopped: apples, pears, any berries, grapes, mandarin oranges, papaya, mango, crushed pineapple (drained)

$\frac{1}{8}$ tsp. vanilla extract

2 tsp.–1 tbs. confectioners' sugar

$\frac{1}{8}$ tsp. cinnamon

2 tsp.–1 tbs. chopped walnuts, optional

fresh fruit, cinnamon or confectioners' sugar for garnish, optional

Mix filling ingredients together while bread is soaking in the egg mixture. Spread filling on unsoaked side of bread, top with a second slice of soaked bread, and cook 2 to 4 minutes. Garnish with fruit and cinnamon or sugar, if desired.

FRENCH TOAST A L'ORANGE

Orange juice adds a little kick to your basic French toast.

Bread: orange raisin, cinnamon raisin swirl, raisin or white

Egg Mixture
1 egg, beaten
1–1½ tbs. orange juice
1–1½ tbs. milk
⅛ tsp. grated orange zest, optional

Filling
2–3 tbs. cream cheese, softened
½–¾ tsp. orange juice
¼–½ tsp. honey

Mix ingredients together for egg mixture. Mix cream cheese, orange juice and honey together while bread is soaking in egg mixture. Spread filling on unsoaked side of bread, top with a second slice of soaked bread, and cook 2 to 4 minutes.

HAWAIIAN FRENCH TOAST

This tropical breakfast treat is a delicious way to start your day.

Bread: white, oatmeal, raisin, raisin nut, cinnamon swirl or nut

Egg Mixture
1 egg, beaten
1–1¹/₂ tbs. milk or cream
1–1¹/₂ tbs. pineapple juice

Filling
4–5 mandarin orange segments and/or
   3–4 tbs. crushed pineapple and/or
   several thin slices banana
1–1¹/₂ tsp. chopped macadamia nuts, optional
mint leaves to taste

Soak bread in egg mixture. Layer with fruit, macadamia nuts, if desired, and mint leaves. Top with a second slice of soaked bread, and cook 2 to 4 minutes.

HOLIDAY FRENCH TOAST

Serve this colorful, easy treat Christmas morning for a joyous start to the day. Some may find that the mint extract is too strong, but you may like that extra spark.

Bread: white, nut, Italian or French

Egg Mixture: 3–4 tbs. eggnog

Filling
1 to 1½ tbs. cream or cottage cheese
1½ to 2 tsp. mint jelly
about 2 drops mint extract, optional
2 to 3 thinly sliced strawberries

Soak bread slices in eggnog. Mix cheese, jelly and extract (if desired) together. Spread filling on unsoaked side of bread, top with strawberries, and then with a second slice of soaked bread, and cook 2 to 4 minutes.

CINNAMON "BUNS"

This adaptation of sticky buns is sure to please the child in all of us.

Bread: thickly sliced cinnamon raisin, raisin, orange raisin, white, whole wheat or oatmeal

Topping

1–1½ tbs. melted margarine or butter
⅔–1 tsp. cinnamon
2 tsp.–1 tbs. brown sugar
1½–2 tsp. chopped nuts

Glaze, optional:

1½ tbs. powdered sugar
¼ tsp. milk
1 drop vanilla extract

Mix filling ingredients together and spread on one slice of bread. Cook 2 to 4 minutes. Mix glaze ingredients together and glaze if desired.

ALMOND PASTRY

Almonds add crunch to this easy treat.

Wrapper: puff pastry; crescent roll dough; white bread. If using puff pastry or crescent roll dough, add extra filling.

Outside Spread: (white bread only) 1 tbs. melted margarine or butter with a few drops almond extract

Filling

1–1$\frac{1}{2}$ tbs. melted margarine or butter
a few drops almond extract
2 tsp.–1 tbs. brown sugar
2 tsp.–1 tbs. finely chopped almonds

Mix filling and spread on inside of wrapper. Cover with second wrapper. Spread outside of wrappers with margarine mixture if using white bread. Cook 2 to 4 minutes.

BRIE AND ALMONDS

Add 2 or 3 slices of brie cheese.

RAISIN NUT "BUNS"

Try using Craisins (sweetened dried cranberries) instead of raising for a deliciously different flavor.

Wrapper: raisin, cinnamon or white bread; crescent roll dough; puff pastry. If using crescent roll dough or puff pastry, add extra filling.

Filling
1–1½ tbs. melted margarine or butter
2 tsp.–1 tbs. sugar, white or brown
1–1½ tbs. finely chopped walnuts
2–3 tbs. raisins

Mix filling ingredients together and spread on inside of wrapper. Place top wrapper over filling and cook 2 to 4 minutes.

BRIE AND APRICOT PRESERVES

Actually, any fruit preserves would work well in this recipe, but Brie and apricots is a classic combination.

Wrapper: sweet bread; white bread; puff pastry. If using puff pastry, add extra filling.

Filling
2–3 slices Brie cheese
1 tbs. apricot preserves
1–2 tsp. slivered almonds, optional

Layer ingredients on wrapper. Place top wrapper over filling and cook 2 to 4 minutes.

ABOUT PANCAKES

Using your normal pancake batter, fill each scallops to heaping with batter. For machines with two scallops per sandwich, this will be about 3 to 4 tablespoons in each scallop. For makers with one scallop per sandwich, it will be about $1/3$ cup. Cook for about 3 to 4 minutes. About 1 to $1\frac{1}{2}$ minutes into the baking, unlatch the machine so that the pancakes can rise.

ABOUT MUFFINS

Your favorite muffin recipe, whether homemade or purchased mix, may be made in your sandwich maker in just 3 to 4 minutes. Spoon enough batter into the scalloped areas so that it is heaping but not overflowing (3 to 5 large spoonfuls). Bake for about 3 to 4 minutes until a toothpick comes out clean. Start checking the muffins every 30 seconds about 2 minutes into baking as they bake very quickly and could burn easily.

ABOUT QUICK BREADS

Banana, pumpkin, apple and cinnamon breads and a countless variety of quick breads (nonyeast breads) may be baked in your sandwich maker in just a few minutes compared to 30 to 45 minutes of conventional oven baking. Use one of the following or your own favorite recipes, or even a purchased mix, and make the batter as usual. Spoon enough batter into the scallops so that it is heaping but not overflowing (3 to 5 large spoonfuls). Bake for about 3 to 5 minutes until a toothpick inserted into the bread comes out clean. I recommend that you start checking the breads every 30 seconds about 2½ minutes into baking as they bake very quickly and could burn easily. The following quick bread recipes make about 4 to 6 pieces each. Each recipe may be halved (use 1½ tbs. egg substitute for ½ egg) or doubled to fit your needs.

BANANA BREAD

This super-quick bread has real banana flavor.

1 cup mashed ripe banana (about 2 medium)
1 egg
2 tbs. vegetable oil
½ cup sugar
1½ cups self–rising flour
¼–⅓ cup chopped walnuts, optional

Mix wet ingredients together. In a separate bowl, mix dry ingredients together. Combine until just moistened. Follow baking directions on page 29.

PEANUT BUTTER BANANA BREAD

Peanut butter adds a unique twist to banana bread.

¼ cup (½ stick) margarine or butter, softened
½ cup peanut butter
1 cup mashed ripe banana (about 2 medium)
2 eggs
½ tsp. vanilla extract
1 cup brown sugar, packed
2 cups self–rising flour

Mix wet ingredients together. In a separate bowl, mix dry ingredients together. Combine until just moistened. Follow baking directions on page 29.

CORNBREAD

A Southern delight, hot cornbread is a great addition to breakfast, lunch or dinner.

1 cup milk or water

1 egg

2 tbs. vegetable oil

1 tsp. sugar

1 cup cornmeal

1 1/2 cups self–rising flour

Mix wet ingredients together. In a separate bowl, mix dry ingredients together. Combine until just moistened. Follow baking directions on page 29.

ORANGE BREAD

Orange bread is a great bread for holiday-time brunches or entertaining.

2/3 cup orange juice

2/3 cup vegetable oil

1 egg

1/2–1 tsp. grated orange peel, or to taste

1 2/3 cups sugar

2 cups self–rising flour

1/4–1/3 cup chopped walnuts, optional

Mix wet ingredients together. In a separate bowl, mix dry ingredients together. Combine until just moistened. Follow baking directions on page 29.

STRAWBERRY OR PEACH BREAD

Personalize this recipe by using your favorite fruit preserves.

1/3 cup milk
2/3 cup strawberry or peach preserves
3 eggs
1/2 tsp. vanilla extract
1/2 cup (1 stick) butter or margarine, softened
1/2 cup sugar
2/3 cup oats
1 1/3 cups self–rising flour
1/4–1/3 cup chopped walnuts, optional

Mix wet ingredients together. In a separate bowl, mix dry ingredients together. Combine until just moistened. Follow baking directions on page 29.

Note: Half 1/3 cup is roughly 2 1/2 tbs., if you wish to make only half of this recipe.

EGG SANDWICHES

If serving egg sandwiches for a brunch or breakfast, prepare plain scrambled eggs and set out bowls of chopped cheese, meats, veggies or fruit. Eggs need not be kept warm as they will be reheated in the sandwich maker; however, they should not sit too long.

Additional ingredients

cheeses Swiss, fontina, Gruyère, herbed cream cheese, cheddar, American, Parmesan, jalapeño cheese, Monterey Jack, Muenster, feta

cooked meats ham, chicken, turkey, crabmeat, sausage, bacon, lobster, corned beef hash

cooked vegetables onions, bell peppers, hot peppers, asparagus, broccoli, spinach, mushrooms, corn, jalapeños

fruits strawberries and other berries, cranberry sauce, peaches, pears, apples, papaya, banana, jam or jelly

seasonings salt and pepper; fresh or dried marjoram, oregano, sage, tarragon, basil, mint or dill; salt–free seasoning blends; hot sauce.

Fill wrapper with 2 to 3 tbs. scrambled eggs and 1 to 2 tbs. ingredients from above list. Place top wrapper over filling and cook 2 to 4 minutes.

ABOUT OMELETS

Making omelets in the sandwich maker is as easy as spooning the beaten egg into the scallops. Either mix the additions in with the beaten egg and spoon into the scallops, or place filling ingredients in the scallops and spoon lightly beaten eggs on top. These cook quickly and hold their shape well.

Use about ¼ cup (4 tbs.) of beaten egg and extras combined, until level with the scallop edge. Do not clamp the machine closed. Seasonings (salt, pepper and spices or herbs) should be added according to your personal taste. You can also use ingredients listed in Egg Sandwiches, previous page, and make up your own.

HUEVOS RANCHEROS
beaten egg
salsa
jalapeño cheese

cilantro
salt and pepper

HUNGARIAN OMELET

beaten egg

diced onion

diced green pepper

diced ham and salami

salt and pepper

BLUE CHEESE AND ONION OMELET

beaten egg

diced red onion

cooked and crumbled bacon or bacon bits

crumbled blue cheese

garlic powder

salt and white pepper

SPINACH OMELET

You can substitute chopped broccoli, asparagus or diced tomatoes for spinach.

beaten egg

mozzarella cheese

cooked, drained spinach

grated Parmesan cheese

garlic powder

basil, salt and pepper

CHILI OMELET

beaten egg
leftover chili
salt and pepper

PEANUT BUTTER AND JELLY OMELET

This idea was given to me by my friend, Steve Vollendorf, who said this was an often requested omelet when he worked at a college restaurant. It really is quite tasty and has become a favorite of mine.

beaten egg
peanut butter
jelly

GRITS OMELET

egg
cheese
cooked seasoned grits

WESTERN OMELET

beaten egg

diced onion

green pepper

cooked, crumbled bacon

salt and pepper

BANANA OMELET

beaten egg

banana slices

cayenne pepper

fresh chopped parsley

salt and pepper

CRAB OMELET

beaten egg

crabmeat

Tabasco Sauce

lemon juice

ITALIAN SAUSAGE AND PEPPERS OMELET

beaten egg

cooked, sliced Italian sausage

sliced or diced red and/or green bell pepper

diced onion

minced garlic

dried oregano

salt and pepper

EGGS BENEDICT

An easy variation of a classic favorite. The Hollandaise Sauce recipe makes enough for two sandwiches.

Bread: white, whole wheat or rye

Filling

1 poached or scrambled egg
1–2 slices cooked Canadian bacon
1–2 slices American or mozzarella cheese

1 1/2–2 tbs. *Hollandaise Sauce*
salt and pepper to taste

On bottom wrapper, layer egg, bacon and cheese. Top with Hollandaise Sauce and season to taste. Place top wrapper over filling and cook 2 to 4 minutes.

HOLLANDAISE SAUCE

1 egg yolk
1 tsp. lemon juice

1/4 tsp. dry mustard
1/4 cup (1/2 stick) melted butter

Combine egg yolk, lemon juice and mustard in a blender or food processor. Add melted butter slowly. Use immediately.

MONTE CRISTO

This classic is a French–toasted ham and cheese sandwich.

Bread: white, whole wheat, oatmeal, cracked wheat, multi–grain, nut or raisin

Egg Mixture
1 egg, beaten
1–1/2 tbs. milk or cream

Filling
Dijon or other mustard
1–2 slices Swiss or Gruyère cheese
1–2 slices ham
1–2 slices Swiss or Gruyère cheese
1–2 slices turkey

Soak outside of bread with egg mixture. Spread mustard on inside of bread. Layer ingredients in the order given. Place top wrapper over filling and cook 2 to 4 minutes.

HAWAIIAN CHICKEN SANDWICH

The fruit makes this a tropical treat.

Wrapper: pizza dough; white, whole wheat, nut or oatmeal bread; puff pastry; crescent roll dough. If using puff pastry or crescent roll dough, add extra filling.

Filling
mayonnaise
2–3 slices cooked chicken or turkey, or 2 to 3 tbs. diced
1–1½ tsp. coconut flakes
3–4 thin slices banana
2–3 thin slices papaya, optional
ground ginger and salt to taste
coconut flakes for garnish, optional

Spread inside of wrapper with mayonnaise. Layer remaining ingredients on wrapper. Place top wrapper over filling and cook 2 to 4 minutes. Garnish with coconut flakes if desired.

CHICKEN WALDORF

Substitute Craisins (sweetened, dried cranberries) for raisins for a new twist on an old favorite.

Bread: white, whole wheat, cracked wheat, multi–grain, nut or oatmeal

Filling

2–3 tbs. cooked, diced chicken, or ham or turkey
2 tsp.–1 tbs. mayonnaise
1 tsp. chopped walnuts
1 tsp. raisins
$\frac{1}{8}$ apple, diced
salt and pepper to taste

Mix ingredients together and spread filling on wrapper. Place top wrapper over filling and cook 2 to 4 minutes.

CHICKEN WITH HERBS SANDWICH

If you have fresh herbs, use them — simply triple the amount of dried.

Wrapper: whole wheat, oatmeal, white or sourdough breads; pizza dough

Filling
olive oil
2–3 slices cooked chicken or turkey, or 2–4 tbs. diced
1–2 slices mozzarella
1 slice tomato, optional
$\frac{1}{4}$ tsp. dried basil
$\frac{1}{4}$ tsp. dried tarragon
$\frac{1}{8}$ tsp. coarse black pepper
salt to taste

Coat inside wrapper with olive oil. Layer chicken, cheese and tomato if desired. Sprinkle with seasonings. Place top wrapper over filling and cook 2 to 4 minutes.

ORANGE TURKEY SANDWICH

What a wonderful, no–fuss–no–muss way to use leftover holiday turkey!

Bread: raisin, whole wheat, white or Italian
Outside Spread: margarine or butter mixed with grated orange peel, optional
Filling
mayonnaise, optional
2–3 slices cooked turkey, or 2–3 tbs. diced
1–1$\frac{1}{2}$ tsp. cranberry sauce
$\frac{1}{2}$–$\frac{3}{4}$ tsp. orange marmalade

Spread inside wrapper with mayonnaise if desired. Add turkey and spread with cranberry sauce and marmalade. Place top wrapper over filling and brush outsides with orange butter, if desired. Cook 2 to 4 minutes.

MINTED FRUIT SANDWICH

Try serving this tangy sandwich with a chicken or egg salad.

Wrapper: pizza dough; white, Italian, French, oatmeal, or whole wheat breads; puff pastry. If using puff pastry, add extra filling.

Outside Spread: olive oil seasoned with mint

Filling

1 tsp. olive oil
1/2 tsp. balsamic vinegar
1/3–1/2 tsp. dried mint or 1–1 1/2 tsp. fresh
3–4 tbs. finely chopped fruit (or slices): berries, orange segments, grapes, pineapple, papaya

Coat outside of wrapper with seasoned olive oil. Mix olive oil, vinegar and mint, pour over fruit and toss gently. Spread filling on wrapper. Place top wrapper over filling and cook 2 to 4 minutes.

APPLE AND CHEESE SANDWICH

If you slice the apple before you are ready to use it, sprinkle a little lemon or orange juice over it to prevent browning.

Wrapper: pizza dough; white, cinnamon raisin, raisin or nut bread

Filling
1–2 slices fontina or Swiss cheese
4–5 thin slices apple, peach or pear
cinnamon and sugar to taste

Layer cheese and apple slices on wrapper. Sprinkle with cinnamon and sugar. Place top wrapper over filling and cook 2 to 4 minutes.

PINEAPPLE DANISH

This is especially good as an accompaniment to ham.

Wrapper: pizza dough; white, Italian or French bread; crescent roll dough; puff pastry. If using puff pastry or crescent roll dough, add extra filling.

Filling	Single	Multiple
crushed pineapple	1 1/3–1 1/2 tbs.	1/2 cup
plain yogurt	1 1/3–1 1/2 tbs.	1/2 cup
sugar	1/8 tsp.	3/4 tsp.
ground ginger	pinch	1/4 tsp.
vanilla extract	1/8 tsp.	3/4 tsp.
banana	3–4 thin slices	1 banana, thinly sliced
confectioners' sugar for garnish, optional		

Mix together pineapple, yogurt, sugar, ginger and vanilla. Fill wrapper with 3 to 4 tbs. of mixture and add a layer of banana slices. Place top wrapper over filling and cook 2 to 4 minutes. Garnish with confectioners' sugar, if desired.

PINEAPPLE MACADAMIA SANDWICH

You'll think you are in Hawaii when you eat this! The multiple recipe makes 4 to 5 sandwiches or 20 to 24 appetizers.

Wrapper: puff pastry; crescent roll dough; rye, white, pumpernickel or Russian black bread. If using puff pastry or crescent roll dough, add extra filling.

Filling	Single	Multiple
crushed pineapple, drained	1 1/2–2 tbs.	1/2 cup
cream cheese, softened	1 1/2–2 tbs.	4 oz.(1/2 cup)
Tabasco Sauce	1 drop	several drops
macadamia nuts, chopped	1–1 1/2 tsp.	1/4 cup

Mix ingredients together and spread each wrapper with about 3 to 4 tbs. of mixture. Place top wrapper over filling and cook 2 to 4 minutes.

FRUIT QUESADILLAS

Pourable fruit may be found in some large grocery stores, gourmet shops or health food stores. Syrup may be substituted but has sugar which the pourable fruit does not.

Wrapper: pizza dough; white bread; crepes; tortillas; puff pastry. If using crepes, tortillas or puff pastry, add extra filling.

Filling
1½–2 tbs. grated Monterey Jack cheese
1½–2 tbs. fresh fruit, sliced or diced: apples, pears, any berries, grapes, mandarin oranges
1–1½ tsp. pourable fruit
1–1½ tsp. coconut flakes
fruit and coconut flakes for garnish

Place cheese on wrapper. Add fresh fruit and top with pourable fruit and coconut flakes. Place top wrapper over filling and cook 2 to 4 minutes. Garnish with more fruit and coconut if desired.

ORANGE BRIE SANDWICH

Brie and fruit is always a popular combo. You can substitute peaches or papaya for the orange segments.

Wrapper: pizza dough; white bread; puff pastry; crescent roll dough. If using puff pastry or crescent roll dough, add extra filling.

Filling
3–4 slices Brie cheese, herb or regular
4–5 mandarin orange segments
cinnamon, nutmeg or mint to taste

Layer slices of Brie and orange segments on wrapper. Add cinnamon or mint as desired. Place top wrapper over filling and cook 2 to 4 minutes.

FRUITED CHEESE BLINTZ

Everyone loves a good blintz. This multiple recipe is for a group (4 to 5) and is easily divided or multiplied to meet your requirements.

Wrapper: crepes; puff pastry; crescent roll dough; white bread. If using crepes, puff pastry or crescent roll dough, add extra filling.

Filling

4 oz. ($^1/_2$ cup) cream cheese, softened
$^1/_2$ cup cottage cheese
1 tbs. honey
$^1/_4$–$^1/_2$ cup sliced or diced fruit
sliced fruit sprinkled with confectioners' sugar for garnish, optional

Mix cream cheese, cottage cheese and honey thoroughly. Place about 2 to 4 tbs. of filling on each wrapper, topped with about 1$^1/_2$ tbs. fruit. Place top wrapper over filling and cook 2 to 4 minutes. Garnish with slices of fruit sprinkled with confectioners' sugar if desired.

CHICKEN CHEESE PUFF

What an easy way to enjoy cheese puffs! This recipe makes two but is easily multiplied. No wrapper is required.

¹/₄ cup (¹/₂ stick) margarine or butter, softened
1 cup grated cheddar cheese
¹/₂ cup cooked, diced chicken or turkey
2 tbs. milk
1 egg
¹/₂ cup all-purpose flour
¹/₈ tsp. salt
¹/₈ tsp. white pepper or black pepper

Combine all ingredients and mix well. Refrigerate for 30 minutes or longer. Place half the dough at a time in the machine. Bake for about 5 to 7 minutes.

SAUSAGE AND APPLE SANDWICH

This could be an appetizer or a side sandwich for brunch with a green salad.

Bread: whole wheat, oatmeal, multi–grain, apple, herb, white or rye

Filling

$1/2$ tsp. lemon juice or orange juice
4–5 thin slices apple
2–3 tbs. sausage, cooked, drained and crumbled
cinnamon and sugar to taste

Pour lemon or orange juice over apples. Spread sausage over wrapper, cover with apple slices and sprinkle with cinnamon and sugar. Place top wrapper over filling and cook 2 to 4 minutes.

MACADAMIA AND CHEESES SANDWICH

The unusual combination of these two cheeses with macadamias is rich and elegant.

Wrapper: Russian black, pumpernickel bread; pizza dough; white bread

Filling

3–4 slices Brie
1½–2 tsp. chopped macadamia nuts
2 tsp.–1 tbs. blue cheese, crumbled

Layer slices of Brie over bottom wrapper. Sprinkle with nuts and blue cheese. Place top wrapper over filling and cook 2 to 4 minutes.

TEMPTING APPETIZERS

Appetizers are easily made in sandwich makers with two triangular scallops. Halfway through the heating process, give the sandwich a quarter turn so the machine cuts each of the triangles in half. This will seal one sandwich into four appetizers. If your machine makes a single sandwich, cut the sandwich into triangles after it is completed.

Many of the sandwiches in *Favorite Lunch Sandwiches,* pages 69–129, are also possible appetizer fare, for those times when you have guests coming and wish to have before–dinner cocktails. And don't forget the selections in this chapter when you have a snack attack!

CRAB EXTRAORDINAIRE

Your guests won't believe how easy this sophisticated sandwich is to prepare! The recipe makes enough filling for several appetizers.

Bread: rye, pumpernickel or Russian black

Filling

2/3 cup crabmeat
4 oz. (1/2 cup) cream cheese
2 tsp.–1 tbs. salsa
1 1/4 tsp. water
1/4–1/3 tsp. lemon juice
1 tsp. dried cilantro or 1 tbs. chopped fresh
    cilantro
salt and pepper to taste

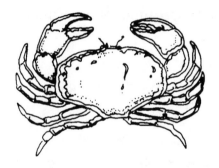

Mix ingredients together until well blended. Fill each wrapper with 3 to 4 tbs. of filling. Place top wrapper over filling and cook 2 to 4 minutes.

You can also serve filling as a dip with vegetables or crackers.

CHEESY TACO APPETIZERS

Stand back and watch how quickly these disappear. This recipe is easily halved or doubled. Makes 24–28 appetizers.

Wrapper: tortillas; white bread; pizza dough. If using tortillas, add extra filling.

Outside Spread: olive oil with cilantro or parsley

Filling
$1/2$ lb. ground beef
$1/2$ pkg. taco seasoning
$1/2$ cup sour cream
$1/2$ cup grated cheddar cheese
fresh or dried cilantro to taste
fresh chopped cilantro or parsley for garnish

Cook ground beef; drain well and mix in taco seasoning and water according to package directions. Simmer until excess liquid evaporates. Combine mixture with remaining ingredients and spread each wrapper with 3 to 4 tbs. of mixture. Place top wrapper over filling. Brush outside of wrapper with seasoned olive oil. Cook 2 to 4 minutes. Garnish with cilantro.

QUICK AND EASY NACHOS

This recipe makes about 64 appetizers. Ro–Tel, a combination of diced tomatoes and green chiles, is usually found either with Mexican foods or canned tomatoes in your grocery store. You can substitute salsa if you wish.

Wrapper: tortillas; white bread; cornbread. If using tortillas, add extra filling.

Filling
1 lb. Velveeta cheese, sliced, or cheddar cheese, grated
1 can (10 oz.) Ro–Tel, partially drained
refried beans, canned, optional
olives, sliced, optional
chopped jalapeño peppers, diced or sliced, optional
cooked, diced chicken or beef, or shredded, optional

Layer cheese (use 1 to 2 slices of Velveeta or 1 to 2 tbs. grated cheddar) with 1 tbs. Ro-Tel and 1 to 3 tbs. of optional ingredients. Place top wrapper over filling and cook 2 to 4 minutes.

CREAM CHEESE CHICKEN TRIANGLES

A hot, spicy appetizer is just the ticket with a cool drink. This recipes makes 16–20 appetizers.

Wrapper: rye, pumpernickel or Russian black bread; pizza dough; puff pastry; crescent roll dough. If using puff pastry or crescent roll dough, add extra filling.

Filling

Dijon or spicy mustard
$1/4$ cup cooked, diced chicken or turkey
4 oz. ($1/2$ cup) cream cheese, softened
1–2 jalapeño peppers, sliced or diced, or 1 tbs. salsa
$1/2$ tsp. dried chives or $1^1/2$ tsp. diced green onion

Spread inside of each wrapper with mustard. Mix remaining ingredients together and spread each wrapper with 3 to 4 tbs. of mixture. Place top wrapper over filling and cook 2 to 4 minutes.

SEAFOOD APPETIZERS

This is a must for those who live in seafood territory. Use canned seafood if fresh is not available. Makes 32–36 appetizers.

Wrapper: Russian black, pumpernickel or dark rye bread; puff pastry; pizza dough. If using puff pastry, add extra filling.

Filling

2/3 cup crabmeat

1/2 cup cooked, chopped shrimp

4 oz. (1/2 cup) cream cheese

1 tbs. sherry

1 tsp. lemon juice

1 tsp. diced onion

1/2 tsp. horseradish

1/2 tsp. Dijon mustard

1/4 cup chopped walnuts, almonds or macadamia nuts

salt and pepper to taste

Mix ingredients together and spread each wrapper with about 3 to 4 tbs. of filling. Place top wrapper over filling and cook 2 to 4 minutes.

PEANUT CHICKEN TIDBITS

A quick and very easy adaptation of an Indonesian saté. Makes about 48 appetizers.

Bread: pita (split and cut to fit), white, whole wheat, nut or raisin

Peanut Sauce

1/2 cup peanut butter
1/4 cup coconut milk
1/4 cup chicken broth
1 tsp. soy sauce
1 tbs. salsa

1/2 clove garlic, minced, or 1/8 tsp. garlic powder
pinch ground ginger
1–2 drops Tabasco Sauce
salt and pepper to taste

Filling

Peanut Sauce (above)

2 cups cooked, diced chicken

Mix sauce ingredients together. Toss chicken in sauce and spread wrapper with 3 to 4 tbs. of mixture. Place top wrapper over filling and cook 2 to 4 minutes.

Note: Coconut milk and broth may be increased to about 1/2 cup each for a thinner sauce and used as a salad dressing or a sauce over grilled chicken.

MACADAMIA COCONUT CHEESE PUFFS

These morsels are crunchy, creamy and rich. The recipe makes 12–16 appetizers.

Wrapper: Russian black, pumpernickel or dark rye bread; pizza dough; puff pastry. If using puff pastry, add extra filling.

Filling
4 oz. (1/2 cup) cream cheese, softened
1/4 cup chopped macadamia nuts
2 tbs. coconut flakes
pinch cinnamon

Mix ingredients together until well blended. Fill each wrapper with 3 to 4 tablespoons of mixture. Place top wrapper over filling and cook 2 to 4 minutes.

HAM AND CREAM CHEESE COCKTAIL BITES

A simple ham and cheese sandwich, all dressed up for a party. This recipe makes 20–24 appetizers.

Wrapper: Russian black, pumpernickel or dark rye bread;, pizza dough; puff pastry. If using puff pastry, add extra filling.

Filling
4 oz. ($1/2$ cup) cream cheese, softened
$1/4$ cup grated cheddar cheese
$1/2$ cup diced ham
$1/2$ green onion, chopped, or $1/4$ tsp. dried chives
$1/2$ tsp. mustard
2 tbs. chopped walnuts

Mix ingredients together and spread wrapper with 3 to 4 tbs. of mixture. Place top wrapper over filling and cook 2 to 4 minutes.

QUESADILLAS

Quesadillas are normally cheese–filled tortillas heated until the cheese melts. It is very common to find any and all types of ingredients added to them. Use your imagination and combine whatever looks good. Cilantro can be found with spices (dried), or in the produce section (fresh herb). This recipe makes 12–16 appetizers.

Wrapper: tortillas; white or whole wheat bread. If using tortillas, add extra filling.
Outside Spread: vegetable oil or olive oil

Filling

$1/2$ cup grated Monterey Jack cheese
1 tomato, diced
$1-1\frac{1}{2}$ tbs. diced green bell pepper
$1-1\frac{1}{2}$ tbs. diced onion

$1/4$ cup salsa
fresh or dried cilantro to taste, optional
salt and pepper to taste
salsa for garnish

Combine ingredients and spread wrapper with 3 to 4 tbs. of mixture. Top with second wrapper and coat outside of wrapper with oil. Cook 2 to 4 minutes.

For variety, add sliced mushrooms, green beans, or broccoli; diced cooked meats such as turkey or chicken, or cooked ground meats.

CRAB QUESADILLAS

If you like crabmeat and Mexican food, you'll love this. Makes 12–16 appetizers.

Wrapper: tortillas; white or whole wheat bread. If using tortillas, add extra filling.

Outside Spread: vegetable oil or olive oil, optional

Filling
1/2 cup grated Monterey Jack cheese
1/4 cup crabmeat (or cooked, diced shrimp)
1 tbs. diced green onion or 1 tsp. dried chives
1/2 clove garlic, minced, or 1/8 tsp. garlic powder
1/8 tsp. Tabasco Sauce
1/4 tsp. lemon juice
fresh or dried cilantro to taste, optional
salt and pepper to taste

Toss ingredients together and spread wrapper with 3 to 4 tbs. of mixture. Top with second wrapper. Coat outside of wrapper with oil if desired. Cook 2 to 4 minutes. For variety, substitute cheddar or American cheese for the Monterey Jack.

GREEK SPINACH AND FETA APPETIZERS

Serve this with a Greek salad for a great lunch. I cook spinach and keep it sealed in the refrigerator for a few days so it's on hand for snacks like this. Makes 12–16.

Wrapper: pita (split and cut to fit); pizza dough; white or Italian bread

Outside Spread: olive oil with parsley or dill, optional

Filling

olive oil
1/4 cup spinach, cooked, drained and chopped
3 tbs. crumbled feta cheese
1/4 cup grated mozzarella cheese

3/4 tsp. minced grated onion
1 tsp. dried parsley or 1 tbs. chopped fresh
1/2 clove garlic, minced, or 1/8 tsp. garlic powder

Spread olive oil inside wrapper. Combine remaining ingredients and spread wrapper with 3 to 4 tbs. of mixture. Top with second wrapper. Brush seasoned oil on outside of wrappers if desired. Cook 2 to 4 minutes.

SPINACH AND TOMATO FETA APPETIZERS

Substitute one slice of tomato per wrapper for mozzarella and dill for parsley.

GREEK CHEESE TURNOVERS

This is based on a recipe for tirópeta, cheese turnovers baked in phyllo. Makes 12–16 appetizers.

Wrapper: white bread; phyllo; puff pastry. If using phyllo or puff pastry add extra filling.

Filling
olive oil
1/2 cup cottage cheese
3 tbs. crumbled feta cheese
3/4 tsp. dried chives or 1 tbs. finely chopped green onion
2 tsp. dried parsley or 2 tbs. fresh, parsley optional

Spread olive oil inside wrapper. Mix ingredients together and spread wrapper with 3 to 4 tbs. of mixture. Place top wrapper over filling and cook 2 to 4 minutes.

EGYPTIAN MINTED RICE TRIANGLES

This is an adaptation of an Egyptian recipe which is stuffed into vine leaves and steamed. This is enough for 12–16 appetizers a — great use for leftover rice!

Wrapper: herb, mint or white bread; pizza dough

Outside Spread: olive oil with mint or parsley

Filling

1/2 cup cooked rice
1 1/2–2 tbs. cup finely chopped onion
1/4 cup spaghetti sauce
1–2 tbs. raisins, optional
1/2 tsp. dried parsley or 1 1/2 tsp. fresh parsley
1 tsp. dried mint or 1 tbs. fresh mint
salt and pepper to taste

Mix ingredients together and spread wrapper with about 3 to 4 tbs. of mixture. Top with second wrapper. Brush outside of wrapper with seasoned olive oil. Cook 2 to 4 minutes.

SPINACH, CHEESE AND CHICKEN BITES

Water chestnuts add crunch to these savory bites. Makes 12–16 appetizers.

Bread: white, whole wheat, cracked wheat, rye, pumpernickel or Russian black

Outside Spread: olive oil with basil or oregano, optional

Filling

$1/4$ cup ricotta cheese
$1/3$ cup cooked, drained, chopped spinach
4 tbs. grated Parmesan cheese
$1/2$ cup cooked, diced chicken or turkey
2 tbs. chopped water chestnuts
$1/8$ tsp. garlic powder
fresh or dried oregano and basil to taste
salt and pepper to taste
fresh chopped parsley for garnish, optional

Mix ingredients together. Spread 3 to 4 tbs. filling on each wrapper. Top with second wrapper. Brush outside of wrapper with seasoned olive oil if desired. Cook 2 to 4 minutes. Garnish with parsley if desired.

FAVORITE LUNCH SANDWICHES

Lunch, for most people, is a quick sandwich on the run. These recipes are not only deliciously tasty but are also quick and easy to prepare. At most, ingredients need to be mixed together prior to placing on the bread.

Some of the easiest, most common sandwiches such as peanut butter and jelly, ham and cheese or even a basic tomato sandwich have unlimited variations. Hopefully, the lists of variations I include along with the recipes will spark your tastebuds and your imagination.

PEANUT BUTTER AND JELLY — AND VARIATIONS

In addition to the garden variety peanut butter and jelly or preserves that we all use, other nut and fruit butters are available in gourmet shops, some larger groceries, or by mail order, or you can make your own butters. For nut butter, place 1 cup roasted nuts in a food processor with a steel blade. Process a few minutes until it changes from chopped nuts to a thick paste. A touch of peanut or vegetable oil may be added during the processing if needed. The butter will firm during refrigeration. Keep tightly covered in the refrigerator for about 1 to 1½ weeks.

I've included some cream cheese and cottage cheese sandwiches in this section because they are made in such a similar way. Another method of varying plain peanut butter and jelly is to vary the bread itself. Try apple oatmeal bread, raisin bread, cinnamon raisin bread or whole wheat raisin cinnamon.

- peanut butter and cream cheese
- peanut butter and cottage cheese (with or without raisins and/or banana)
- peanut butter and raisins
- peanut butter and applesauce
- peanut butter and banana, apple or pear slices

- cream cheese and jelly
- peanut butter and marshmallow creme – a favorite of kids and very sweet
- cream cheese and chutney
- cream cheese and pimientos
- cream cheese or cottage cheese and cranberry sauce or Craisins
- peanut butter, cottage cheese, walnuts, raisins, cinnamon and nutmeg
- cottage cheese, fruit, vanilla extract and sugar to taste
- peanut butter or cream/cottage cheese and mandarin orange segments (with or without coconut flakes)
- hazelnut butter and orange marmalade
- almond butter with peach marmalade/jam
- peanut butter with apple butter

HAM AND CHEESE SANDWICH VARIATIONS

Use your favorite spreads such as mayonnaise, mustard, even Russian or Thousand Island dressings. Try different mustards to vary your sandwiches a little. As always, try different breads from white to Russian black bread. Season with spices, salt–free seasoning blends and/or salt and pepper. Experiment with additions of sliced tomato, diced onion, or jalapeños.

- Virginia ham and Brie
- prosciutto or country ham and fontina cheese
- prosciutto or country ham and mozzarella cheese
- Black Forest or smoked ham and Brie
- Black Forest or smoked ham and Muenster cheese (with or without turkey)
- Black Forest or smoked ham and Jarlsberg cheese

TOMATO AND CHEESE VARIATIONS

There is nothing better than fresh tomatoes in sandwiches. Fresh herbs really add the best flavors but dried are good too! An absolutely superb seasoning for all tomato sandwiches is olive oil seasoned with basil, oregano, marjoram, dill or mint, or even, for a little zest, cilantro (a.k.a. coriander leaves or Chinese parsley). Keep a container of premixed olive oil with your favorite spice on hand. Coat the inside and/or outside of the bread. Mayonnaise is always a good inside spread, also.

- tomato, mozzarella, feta or provolone cheese, olive oil seasoned with basil
- tomato and mozzarella cheese with bacon, ham, chicken, turkey or tuna
- tomato and blue cheese or herbed cream cheese
- tomato, cheddar and jalapeño slices
- tomato and blue cheese or herbed cream cheese
- add 1 to 2 spears of cooked or canned asparagus
- add 1 to 2 tbs. cooked, chopped broccoli florets
- add 1 to 2 tbs. finely diced red onion and season with mustard
- substitute zucchini (slightly cooked) for the tomato and season with garlic powder, basil and oregano

EASY COMBOS

Season your sandwiches with salt and pepper, or try some of the premixed salt–free seasoning blends. The blends may specify which meats or foods they go best with. Use your favorite mayonnaise and/or mustard or try new, different mustards.

- roast beef, provolone cheese, horseradish, mayonnaise
- roast beef, Swiss cheese, coleslaw, mayonnaise
- roast beef, mashed potatoes, gravy (a great way to finish the leftovers!)
- corned beef, pastrami, coleslaw, Dijon mustard
- corned beef, pastrami, brisket, Swiss cheese, tomato, Dijon mustard
- Polish kielbasa, havarti, mustard
- tuna or chicken salad with diced jalapeños and cheddar
- turkey, pastrami, Swiss cheese, oregano to taste
- turkey, salami, Monterey Jack cheese, mayonnaise and/or mustard
- turkey, prosciutto, Swiss or Gruyère cheese, red onion, oregano, mayonnaise or olive oil
- turkey with blue cheese, mayonnaise
- chicken salad with Craisins and gouda

ZUCCHINI AND TOMATO SANDWICH

Can you imagine anything better than zucchini, tomatoes and herbs fresh from your garden in a sandwich like this?

Bread: whole wheat, rye, pumpernickel, cracked wheat or multi–grain

Filling

1½–2 tsp. olive oil
fresh chopped oregano and/or basil to taste
3–4 thin slices zucchini, cooked
1 slice tomato
1 tsp. diced onions, optional
1 slice Muenster cheese
salt and pepper to taste

Coat inside of bread with seasoned oil. Layer remaining ingredients. Place top wrapper over filling and cook 2 to 4 minutes.

For variety, add cooked, crumbled bacon or cooked, diced chicken or turkey.

THE ULTIMATE TURKEY SANDWICH

Make this on sweet potato bread and you have an entire Thanksgiving meal! I have been known to roast a turkey just to have leftovers for sandwiches like this.

Bread: whole wheat, 7–grain or multi–grain, cracked wheat, white, potato, sweet potato, rye, pumpernickel or cranberry

Filling
mayonnaise
1–2 slices cooked turkey, or 1–2 tbs. diced
1–1½ tbs. turkey dressing
1–1½ tbs. cranberry sauce
salt and pepper to taste

Spread mayonnaise inside slices of bread. Layer turkey, dressing and cranberry sauce and season. Place top wrapper over filling and cook 2 to 4 minutes.

SHRIMP AND PROSCIUTTO SANDWICH

Mild, sweet shrimp and spicy prosciutto are a match made in heaven.

Bread: whole wheat, rye, pumpernickel, cracked wheat, multi–grain or white

Outside Spread: olive oil with basil, optional

Filling
mustard
1–2 slices prosciutto or country ham
3–5 cooked, diced shrimp
1–2 slices mozzarella cheese, or 1–2 tbs. grated
1–1½ slices tomato
pinch garlic powder
fresh or dried basil to taste
salt and pepper to taste

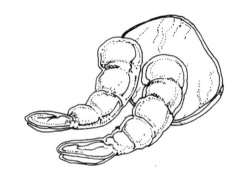

Spread mustard inside slices of bread, and layer ham, shrimp, cheese and tomato. Sprinkle with garlic powder, basil, salt and pepper. Top with second slice of bread. Coat outside of bread with seasoned olive oil if desired. Cook 2 to 4 minutes.

CHICKEN AND CUCUMBER SANDWICH

If you have never tried cucumbers in a sandwich before, you are in for a real treat.

Bread: whole wheat, rye, pumpernickel or white

Filling

Italian salad dressing
2–3 slices cooked chicken or turkey, or 2–3 tbs. diced
3–4 slices cucumber
1–2 slices mozzarella cheese
1–1½ tsp. chopped walnuts
salt–free seasoning blend to taste

Spread Italian salad dressing inside slices of bread. Layer chicken, cucumber and cheese; sprinkle with walnuts and seasoning blend. Place top wrapper over filling and cook 2 to 4 minutes.

ORANGE CHICKEN SANDWICH

Citrus provides a tangy accent to chicken and cheese.

Bread: whole wheat, rye, white, sourdough, raisin or nut

Filling

mayonnaise
1–2 slices chicken or turkey
1–2 slices mozzarella cheese, optional
2–3 orange segments
fresh or dried cilantro or salt–free seasoning blend to
   taste

Spread inside of bread slices with mayonnaise. Layer chicken, cheese and orange segments on wrapper. Sprinkle with cilantro or seasoning blend. Place top wrapper over filling and cook 2 to 4 minutes.

REUBEN SANDWICH

Who can resist a Reuben on a clear, fall football day?

Bread: rye or pumpernickel

Filling
Thousand Island or Russian dressing, or Dijon mustard
1–2 slices Swiss cheese
2–3 slices corned beef
1–2 slices pastrami, optional
1–1½ tbs. sauerkraut

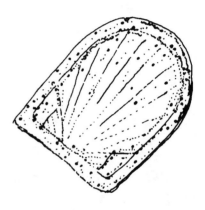

Spread inside of bread slices with dressing. Layer remaining ingredients in the order given. Place top wrapper over filling and cook 2 to 4 minutes.

JICAMA AND HAM SANDWICH

Jicama is a very crunchy, tasty root vegetable. It looks like an overgrown potato and can be found in some well-stocked grocery stores or Mexican stores. Cut off what you need and refrigerate the rest. Try it in any of your favorite sandwiches for added crunch. A bonus: it's very low in calories!

Bread: rye, pumpernickel or whole wheat

Filling
herbed or spicy mustard
1–2 slices ham
1–2 slices provolone or mozzarella cheese
2–3 tbs. peeled, diced jicama

Spread inside slices of bread with mustard. Layer ham and cheese; sprinkle with diced jicama. Place top wrapper over filling and cook 2 to 4 minutes.

BROCCOLI, CHEESE AND CHICKEN SANDWICH

Chicken and broccoli seem to complement each other so well in many dishes, why not a sandwich too?

Bread: white, whole wheat, oregano, pepper, Italian or French

Outside Spread: olive oil seasoned with basil or dill, optional

Filling
olive oil
1–2 slices cooked chicken or turkey, or 1–2 tbs. diced
2–3 slices mozzarella or provolone cheese, or 2–3 tbs. grated
1–2 tbs. cooked, chopped broccoli
pinch garlic powder
fresh or dried basil or dill to taste
salt and pepper to taste

Brush inside of bread with olive oil. Layer chicken and cheese; sprinkle with broccoli. Add garlic powder and seasonings. Cover with second slice of bread. Coat outside of bread with seasoned olive oil if desired. Cook 2 to 4 minutes.

CUBAN SANDWICH

Here is one of the many tasty Cuban sandwiches found throughout Florida.

Bread: Cuban, French, Italian or white

Filling
mustard
1–2 slices ham
1½–2 slices roast pork
1 slice Swiss cheese
1–1½ slices Italian hard salami
1–2 diced pickle, dill or bread and butter
salt and pepper to taste
butter or margarine

Spread mustard inside 1 slice of bread. Layer with ham, pork, cheese and salami. Sprinkle with pickle and seasonings. Butter inside remaining slice of bread. Place top wrapper over filling and cook 2 to 4 minutes.

PROSCIUTTO AND CHEESE SANDWICH

This Italian treat is a little cheesier than a basic ham and cheese.

Bread: whole wheat, cracked wheat, multi–grain, rye, pumpernickel or white

Filling

olive oil, optional
2–3 slices prosciutto or country ham
1–2 slices mozzarella cheese, or 1–1½ tbs. grated
1–1½ tbs. ricotta cheese
2 tsp. grated Parmesan cheese
Italian seasoning or fresh or dried basil and oregano
    to taste
salt and pepper to taste

   Spread olive oil on inside of bread if desired. Layer prosciutto and mozzarella on bread. Top with ricotta and Parmesan cheeses; season to taste. Place top wrapper over filling and cook 2 to 4 minutes.

EASY BEANS SANDWICH

Use your favorite canned beans (I like kidney beans) to personalize this sandwich.

Bread: white, multi–grain, or rye bread; tortillas; pizza dough

Filling
2–3 tbs. canned or cooked beans, rinsed and drained
1 tbs. diced onion
1 tbs. diced jalapeño pepper
1–2 tbs. grated cheddar cheese
salt and pepper to taste

Mix ingredients together and spread on wrapper. Place top wrapper over filling and cook 2 to 4 minutes.

For variety, omit the onions and jalapeño and add 1 tbs. salsa.

SMOKED TURKEY AND BRIE SANDWICH

Mustard gives this sandwich a little pizzazz.

Wrapper: white, whole wheat, cracked wheat, pumpernickel or black bread; pizza dough

Filling
honey mustard or spicy mustard
2–3 slices smoked turkey
3–4 slices Brie
1 slice tomato
salt–free seasoning blend to taste

Spread mustard on inside of wrapper. Layer remaining ingredients. Place top wrapper over filling and cook 2 to 4 minutes.

For variety, substitute 1 or 2 slices of provolone cheese for Brie.

PROSCIUTTO AND PEACHES SANDWICH

Fresh peaches are wonderful but frozen or canned may be used too.

Bread: whole wheat, cracked wheat, oatmeal, multi–grain, white or sourdough

Outside Spread: olive oil seasoned with fresh chopped parsley

Filling
2–4 slices prosciutto or country ham
1–2 slices provolone or mozzarella cheese
3–4 thin peach slices
chopped parsley to taste

Layer prosciutto, cheese and peach slices on one slice of bread; sprinkle with parsley. Top with second slice. Coat outside of bread slices with seasoned olive oil. Cook 2 to 4 minutes.

For variety, substitute pears or apples for peaches.

SPICY CLUB SANDWICH

If you like zesty food, you'll love this one.

Wrapper: white, oatmeal, whole wheat or rye bread; tortillas; pizza dough

Outside Spread: olive oil or vegetable oil with fresh chopped parsley

Filling

2–3 slices ham
1–2 slices Monterey Jack or cheddar cheese, or 1–1$\frac{1}{2}$ tbs. grated
1–2 slices cooked chicken or turkey, or 1–2 tbs. diced
salsa to taste
salt and pepper to taste

Layer ham, cheese and chicken on wrapper. Spread with salsa and season to taste. Place top wrapper over filling. Coat outside of wrapper with seasoned oil and cook 2 to 4 minutes.

CROQUE MONSIEUR

This is a speedy variation of the classic French sandwich. Try dipping the bread in an egg-milk mixture before cooking for an authentic Croque Monsieur.

Bread: French, Italian or white

Outside Spread: melted butter

Filling
Dijon mustard
1–2 slices Swiss or Gruyère cheese
2–4 slices ham
1–2 slices Swiss or Gruyère cheese
salt and pepper to taste

Spread inside of bread slices with Dijon mustard. Layer ingredients in the order given. Add second slice of bread. Coat outside of bread slices witmelted butter. Cook 2 to 4 minutes.

CROQUE MADAME
Substitute chicken for the ham.

HAM AND SALAMI SANDWICH

Some of these old favorites are even better after they're grilled in the sandwich maker.

Bread: whole wheat, rye, multi–grain or white

Outside Spread: olive oil with basil or oregano

Filling

olive oil with basil or oregano

1–2 slices ham

1–2 slices provolone or mozzarella cheese

1–2 slices salami

1 slice tomato, optional

Brush seasoned olive oil inside slices of bread and layer ingredients in order given. Add a second slice of bread. Coat outside of bread slices with seasoned olive oil. Cook 2 to 4 minutes.

For variety, substitute mustard and/or mayonnaise in place of seasoned oil on the inside of sandwich. Spices may still be used with mayonnaise.

BACON, TOMATO, CHICKEN AND CHEESE SANDWICH

Based on a BLT, the lettuce has been left out as it wilts when heated.

Bread: white, whole wheat or rye

Filling

mayonnaise

1½–2 slices bacon, cooked, crumbled

1 slice tomato

1–2 slices cooked chicken or turkey, or 1–2 tbs.
  diced

1–2 slices American, mozzarella or cheddar
  cheese

fresh or dried basil, salt and pepper to taste

Spread mayonnaise inside slices of bread and layer ingredients in order given. Season to taste. Place top wrapper over filling and cook 2 to 4 minutes.

For variety, substitute Russian Dressing for mayonnaise; or use chicken or turkey salad for meat, omitting mayonnaise.

ITALIAN SUB

Take that deli favorite and heat it in the sandwich maker for a true delight. Any three of the meats would be sufficient, or use them all!

Wrapper: Italian, white, French or whole wheat bread; pizza dough

Filling

2 tsp.–1 tbs. olive oil
1–1½ tsp. vinegar
fresh or dried basil to taste
2–3 rings jalapeño pepper, seeded, optional
1–1½ tsp. pimiento, optional
1–2 slices Genoa salami

1–2 slices provolone cheese
1–2 slices capicola ham (Italian)
5–6 slices small slices pepperoni
1–2 slices turkey breast
1 slice tomato

Combine olive oil, vinegar, basil and jalapeños if desired. Coat inside of wrapper with oil mixture and layer remaining ingredients. Place top wrapper over filling and cook 2 to 4 minutes.

PINEAPPLE CHICKEN SANDWICH

An Asian flavor makes this a great change-of-pace.

Wrapper: white or whole wheat bread; pizza dough

Filling

2–3 slices cooked chicken or turkey, or 2–3 tbs. diced

1–1½ tbs. crushed pineapple, well drained
¾–1 tsp. soy sauce
pinch ground ginger

Layer chicken on wrapper and cover with crushed pineapple. Mix soy sauce and ginger and pour over layered ingredients. Place top wrapper over filling and cook 2 to 4 minutes.

CHICKEN AND ONIONS SANDWICH

Sauteed onions add a sweet crunch to this sandwich.

Bread: whole wheat, rye, pumpernickel or white
Filling
mayonnaise or mustard
2–3 slices cooked chicken or turkey
2–3 tbs. finely diced red onion, sautéed
1–1½ tbs. diced red or green pepper
1–1½ tbs. grated mozzarella cheese
½ tsp. dried basil or 1½ tsp. fresh basil

Spread mayonnaise inside slices of bread. Layer chicken slices on one slice. Mix remaining ingredients together and spread on chicken. Place top wrapper over filling and cook 2 to 4 minutes.

PEACHES AND HAM SANDWICH

Peaches, whether fresh or canned, add lots of zip to this sandwich.

Wrapper: pizza dough; whole wheat, cracked wheat, white, nut or herb bread

Filling

olive oil

1–2 slices ham, or 1½–2 tbs. diced

1–2 slices mozzarella cheese,
    or 1½–2 tbs. diced

2–4 thin peach slices

basil to taste

salt-free seasoning blend to taste,
    optional

Brush olive oil on inside of wrapper. Layer ham, mozzarella and peaches. Season to taste. Place top wrapper over filling and cook 2 to 4 minutes.

TUNA MELT SANDWICH

This has always been one of my favorite hot sandwiches. This classic is now adapted to your sandwich makers. This recipe makes enough filling for several sandwiches.

Bread: rye, pumpernickel, whole wheat, cracked wheat, multi–grain, sourdough or white

Filling
1 (9$\frac{1}{4}$ oz.) can tuna, drained
$\frac{1}{4}$ cup mayonnaise or to taste
3 tbs.–$\frac{1}{4}$ cup diced celery or diced pickles
fresh chopped parsley to taste, optional
salt and pepper or salt–free seasoning blend to taste
1–2 slices American, Swiss, Muenster or provolone cheese

Mix tuna, mayonnaise, celery, parsley if desired and seasoning. Spread 3 to 4 tbs. over bread and cover with cheese. Place top wrapper over filling and cook 2 to 4 minutes.

For variety, substitute canned chicken, turkey, or deviled ham for tuna; Italian dressing for mayonnaise.

PIZZA SANDWICH

What an easy way to enjoy pizza. Keep the sauce and mozzarella in the refrigerator for quick throw–togethers. Kids of all ages love these!

Wrapper: pizza dough; white, Italian, French, whole wheat or pepper bread

Outside Spread: olive oil with oregano or basil to taste

Filling

1½–2 tbs. pizza sauce

2–3 tbs. grated mozzarella cheese, or 2–3 slices

1–2 tbs. any of the following, optional: sliced pepperoni, sliced mushrooms, cooked ground beef or sausage, diced peppers, diced onions, or any of your favorite pizza toppings

Mix ingredients together and spread on wrapper. Place top wrapper over filling. Brush outside of wrapper with seasoned olive oil and cook 2 to 4 minutes.

CALZONE

These treats are addictive!

Wrapper: white, oregano, pepper, Italian or French bread; pizza dough

Outside Spread: olive oil with oregano or basil to taste

Filling

1–1½ tbs. ricotta cheese
1–2 slices mozzarella cheese, or 1–1½ tbs. grated
1–2 slices provolone cheese, or 1–1½ tbs. grated
Italian seasonings to taste
salt and pepper to taste

Spread inside wrapper with ricotta, layer with remaining cheeses and season to taste. Top with a second wrapper. Brush seasoned olive oil on outside of wrapper. Cook 2 to 4 minutes.

ITALIAN SAUSAGE AND PEPPERS SANDWICH

A classic sandwich is adapted to fit your sandwich maker.

Wrapper: pizza dough; Italian, French or white bread

Filling

olive oil, optional

2–3 tbs. cooked, drained, diced or sliced Italian sausage, or sliced

1–1½ tsp. chopped onion

2 tsp.–1 tbs. chopped green pepper

1–1½ tbs. spaghetti sauce

1–2 slices mozzarella cheese, or 1–2 tbs. grated

fresh or dried oregano and basil to taste

salt and pepper to taste

Brush olive oil on inside of wrapper if desired. Mix sausage, onion, green pepper and spaghetti sauce and spread over wrapper. Cover with mozzarella and season to taste. Place top wrapper over filling and cook 2 to 4 minutes.

MEATBALL SANDWICH

Who doesn't love a great meatball sandwich?

Wrapper: Italian, white, French or oregano bread; pizza dough

Filling

olive oil, optional
2–3 meatballs, cooked, sliced or quartered
1$\frac{1}{2}$–2 tbs. spaghetti sauce
2–2$\frac{1}{2}$ slices mozzarella cheese, or 2–2$\frac{1}{2}$ tbs. grated
fresh or dried basil and oregano to taste
pinch garlic powder
salt and pepper to taste

Brush inside of wrapper with olive oil if desired. Layer meatballs on wrapper, cover with spaghetti sauce and mozzarella, and season to taste. Place top wrapper over filling and cook 2 to 4 minutes.

LAZY LASAGNA

Replace pasta with bread or pizza dough and you have this quick, easy lasagna.

Wrapper: Italian, French, white, sourdough, oregano or pepper bread; pizza dough

Filling

1–1½ tbs. spaghetti sauce
1–1½ tbs. ricotta or cottage cheese
1–2 slices mozzarella or provolone cheese, or
   1–2 tbs. grated

1–1½ tsp. grated Parmesan cheese
fresh or dried oregano and basil to taste
pinch garlic powder
salt and pepper to taste

Spread wrapper with spaghetti sauce and ricotta. Top with mozzarella, sprinkle with Parmesan and season to taste. Place top wrapper over filling and cook 2 to 4 minutes.

- **SPINACH LASAGNA:** add 1–1½ tbs. cooked spinach, drained and chopped
- **ASPARAGUS LASAGNA:** add 2–3 spears of canned or cooked asparagus
- **ZUCCHINI LASAGNA:** add 2–4 thin slices of cooked zucchini
- **MEAT LASAGNA:** add 1–1½ tbs. cooked, diced ground meat or sausage

JALAPEÑO CHICKEN SANDWICH

This is for the true jalapeño lover.

Wrapper: white, whole wheat or cracked wheat bread; tortillas; pizza dough. If using tortillas, add extra filling.

Filling

2–3 slices cooked chicken or turkey, or 2–3 tbs. diced
1–2 slices jalapeño cheese
1–2 rings jalapeño, or ½–1 tsp. diced, optional
2–3 slices onion, or ½–1 tsp. diced, optional
1–2 tsp. salsa

Layer chicken and cheese on wrapper. Add jalapeño and onion if desired and top with salsa. Place top wrapper over filling and cook 2 to 4 minutes.

ALMOND CHICKEN SANDWICH

Almonds and snow peas add crunch and flavor to this delicious sandwich.

Bread: white, Italian, French, almond, whole wheat, rye or pumpernickel

Filling

mayonnaise
2–3 slices cooked chicken or turkey, or 2–3 tbs. diced
1½–2 tsp. chopped almonds
4–5 snow peas, fresh or frozen and thawed, diced
⅓–½ tsp. chopped onion
pinch garlic powder

Spread inside of bread slices with mayonnaise. Place slices of chicken on bread, top with almonds, snow peas and onion, and season. Place top wrapper over filling and cook 2 to 4 minutes.

CHICKEN CORDON BLEU SANDWICH

This favorite entrée is adapted to a sandwich.

Wrapper: white or French bread; pizza dough; puff pastry; oregano bread. If using puff pastry, add extra filling.

Filling
2–3 tsp. sour cream
1–2 slices cooked chicken or turkey
1–2 slices Swiss cheese
1–2 slices ham
1–1½ tbs. mushrooms, sliced
fresh chopped parsley to taste
pinch onion and garlic powders
salt and pepper to taste

Spread sour cream on inside of wrapper. Layer chicken, cheese, ham and mushrooms. Add parsley and seasonings. Place top wrapper over filling and cook 2 to 4 minutes.

ORIENTAL CHICKEN AND HAM SANDWICH

The sauce gives this sandwich a taste of the Far East. Hoisin sauce is usually found in the Oriental foods section of your grocery store.

Wrapper: pita (split and cut to fit); white bread; pizza dough; Italian or French bread

Sauce

2 tsp. hoisin sauce
$1/8$ tsp. sesame oil
pinch garlic powder

pinch ground ginger
$1/8$ tsp. dried chives

Filling

1–2 slices cooked chicken or turkey,
 or 1–2 tbs. diced

1–2 slices ham or 1–2 tbs. diced
1–2 thinly sliced mushrooms

Combine sauce ingredients and spread on inside of wrapper. Layer chicken, ham and mushrooms over sauce. Place top wrapper over filling and cook 2 to 4 minutes.

ELEGANT CHICKEN SANDWICH

This sandwich is an adaptation of the well-loved chicken casserole.

Wrapper: whole wheat, pumpernickel, multi–grain, white, oatmeal or rye bread; puff pastry. If using puff pastry, add extra filling.

Filling

2–3 slices cooked chicken or turkey, or 2–3 tbs. diced
1–2 slices chipped beef
1–2 strips bacon, cooked, or 1–2 tbs. real bacon bits
1–2 thinly sliced mushrooms
1–1½ tbs. plain yogurt or sour cream
fresh chopped parsley to taste
pinch garlic and onion powders
salt and pepper to taste
paprika to taste

Layer chicken, chipped beef, bacon and mushrooms on wrapper. Top with yogurt and seasonings. Place top wrapper over filling and cook 2 to 4 minutes.

CHICKEN PROSCIUTTO SANDWICH

Salty Italian prosciutto balances nicely with apple in this creative sandwich.

Wrapper: whole wheat, rye or pumpernickel bread; pizza dough

Filling
honey butter
1–2 slices cooked chicken or turkey, or 1–2 tbs. diced
1–2 slices prosciutto or country ham, or 1–2 tbs. diced
1–2 slices cheddar cheese, or 1–1$\frac{1}{2}$ tbs. grated
2–3 thin slices apple
1–1$\frac{1}{2}$ tsp. chopped walnuts or pecans

Spread honey butter on inside of wrapper. Layer chicken, ham, cheddar and apple; sprinkle with nuts. Place top wrapper over filling and cook 2 to 4 minutes.

CHICKEN AND TOMATO SANDWICH

The tomato and green pepper really make this a distinctive sandwich.

Bread: whole wheat, pita (split and cut to fit), oatmeal, rye or pumpernickel

Outside Spread: olive oil seasoned with parsley

Filling

mayonnaise
2–3 slices cooked chicken, ham or turkey, or 2–3 tbs. diced
$1/3$–$1/2$ tsp. diced onion
$2/3$–1 tsp. diced green bell pepper
1 slice tomato
$1/4$–$1/2$ tsp. fresh chopped parsley
salt and pepper to taste

Spread mayonnaise on inside of bread. Layer chicken, onion, green pepper, tomato and parsley. Season to taste. Place top wrapper over filling. Brush outside of wrapper with seasoned oil and cook 2 to 4 minutes.

BROCCOLI AND CHEESE SANDWICH

Serve this as a side dish or as a vegetarian entrée.

Wrapper: white bread; puff pastry; nut bread. If using puff pastry, add extra filling.

Filling
2–4 tbs. cooked chopped broccoli, drained
1–2 slices cheddar or American cheese, or 1–2 tbs. grated
1/4 tsp. caraway seeds
salt and pepper to taste

Arrange chopped broccoli on wrapper. Cover with cheese, sprinkle with caraway seeds and season to taste. Place top wrapper over filling and cook 2 to 4 minutes.

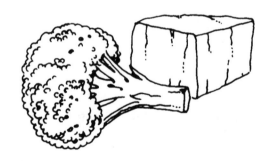

PISTACHIO LAMB SANDWICH

Middle Eastern in flavor, this is a tasty treat.

Wrapper: pita (split and cut to fit); whole wheat or white bread; pizza dough

Filling
olive oil, optional
2–3 tbs. cooked crumbled ground lamb
1–1$\frac{1}{2}$ tbs. spaghetti sauce
1$\frac{1}{2}$–2 tsp. chopped pistachios or pine nuts
salt and pepper to taste

Brush olive oil on inside of wrapper if desired. Mix remaining ingredients together and spread on wrapper. Place top wrapper over filling and cook 2 to 4 minutes.

COCONUT SHRIMP SANDWICH

Coconut makes this an absolutely delicious island sandwich.

Wrapper: rye, pumpernickel, whole wheat or white bread; pizza dough; puff pastry. If using puff pastry, add extra filling.

Filling
1–1$\frac{1}{2}$ tbs. coconut milk
$\frac{1}{2}$–1 tsp. flaked coconut
$\frac{1}{2}$–1 tsp. finely chopped onion
5–8 cooked, chopped shrimp (depends on size) or 2–3 tbs. diced chicken
$\frac{1}{2}$–$\frac{3}{4}$ tsp. finely chopped macadamia nuts

Coat inside of wrapper with coconut milk. Mix remaining ingredients together and spread on wrapper. Place top wrapper over filling and cook 2 to 4 minutes.

SHRIMP AND TOMATO SANDWICH

Tomato and shrimp combine to make a tasty, light sandwich.

Bread: rye, pumpernickel, whole wheat, 7–grain, multi–grain, cracked wheat or white

Outside Spread: olive oil seasoned with fresh chopped parsley or oregano

Filling

mayonnaise
4–8 diced, cooked shrimp
1 slice tomato
1–1½ tbs. crumbled feta cheese
fresh or dried parsley and oregano to taste
salt and pepper to taste

Spread inside of bread with mayonnaise. Cover bread with shrimp, tomato slice and feta. Season to taste. Add top slice of bread. Coat outside of bread with seasoned olive oil. Cook 2 to 4 minutes.

BACON AND SPINACH SANDWICH

This could be served as appetizers, a side dish or a sandwich in its own right.

Bread: rye, pumpernickel or Russian black

Outside Seasoning: olive or vegetable oil with fresh chopped parsley

Filling

2–3 tbs. cooked chopped spinach, drained
1–2 slices bacon, crumbled, or 1–2 tbs. real bacon bits
1½–2 tbs. ricotta cheese
1–3 water chestnuts, sliced or quartered, optional
Vegetable Supreme seasoning to taste or dried basil, parsley and pepper to taste

Mix ingredients together and spread on bread. Top with second slice of bread. Coat outside of bread with seasoned oil. Cook 2 to 4 minutes.

CHEESE AND BACON SANDWICH

Love cheese? This is your kind of sandwich.

Bread: rye, pumpernickel or Russian black

Filling

1–1½ tbs. grated cheddar cheese

1½–2 tbs. cottage cheese

1–2 drops Tabasco Sauce

1–1½ tbs. cooked, crumbled bacon or real
    bacon bits

¼ tsp. dried chives

salt–free seasoning blend to taste

2 tsp.–1 tbs. chopped nuts, optional

   Mix ingredients together and spread on bread. Place top wrapper over filling and cook 2 to 4 minutes.

CINNAMON HAM SANDWICH

What a simple way to vary a basic ham sandwich!

Wrapper: white, whole wheat, cinnamon, raisin or nut bread; pizza dough

Filling

1–1 1/2 tbs. melted butter or margarine
1–1 1/2 tsp. cinnamon
1–1 1/2 tsp. sugar
3–4 slices ham
1–2 slices mozzarella cheese, or 1–1 1/2 tbs. grated

Mix butter, cinnamon and sugar together and coat insides of wrapper. Layer slices of ham and cheese. Place top wrapper over filling and cook 2 to 4 minutes.

HAWAIIAN HAM SANDWICH

Pineapple and ham go hand in hand in sandwiches, too!

Bread: potato, white, whole wheat, rye, cinnamon or nut

Filling
mustard
2–3 slices ham
1–1½ tbs. crushed pineapple, drained
¼–½ tsp. brown sugar

Spread mustard on inside of bread. Layer ham slices and top with crushed pineapple. Sprinkle with brown sugar. Place top wrapper over filling and cook 2 to 4 minutes.

EASY ENTRÉES

Any of the recipes in this chapter provides a quick hot meal for one. Most of these recipes (except for enchiladas) may also be stuffed in a simple pizza dough and baked in your oven. Simply roll out pizza dough (one roll of purchased dough or $1/2$ of the *Pizza Dough* recipe provided on page 6). Spread the filling ingredients on top of that and roll like a jelly roll, starting at the wide end. Pinch ends closed and place seam down on a greased baking sheet. Cover and let rise in a warm, draft-free area for about 30 minutes. Cook in a preheated 350° oven for about 20 to 30 minutes or until golden brown.

CHEESE STEAK

This is based on a Philadelphia cheese steak. Use leftover, thinly sliced steak or purchased steak slices.

Wrapper: white, Italian or whole wheat bread; pizza dough

Outside Spread: olive oil seasoned with oregano

Filling	Single	Multiple
olive oil	1/4–1/2 tsp.	1–1 1/2 tbs.
dried oregano	1/4–1/2 tsp.	1–1 1/2 tbs.
steak, cooked, thinly sliced	2–4 slices	1/2 lb.
American cheese	1–2 slices	1/4 lb. sliced
sautéed onions, optional	1 tbs.	3–4 tbs.
sautéed mushrooms, optional	2 tbs.	1/3 cup
salt and pepper	to taste	to taste

Coat inside of wrapper with olive oil seasoned with oregano. Layer remaining ingredients and season with salt and pepper. Add top wrapper. Coat outside of wrapper with seasoned olive oil. Cook 2 to 4 minutes.

SAUSAGE AND CHEESE SANDWICH

This hearty sandwich is great for picnics or tailgate parties.

Wrapper: Italian, French, white, sourdough, oregano or pepper bread; pizza dough

Outside Spread: olive oil seasoned with fresh chopped parsley

Filling	Single	Multiple
cooked, crumbled sausage	2–3 tbs.	$1/2$ lb.
grated provolone cheese	1–1$1/2$ tbs.	$1/4$ lb.
grated mozzarella cheese	1–1$1/2$ tbs.	$1/4$ lb.
garlic powder	to taste	$1/4$–$1/2$ tsp.
salt and pepper	to taste	to taste

Mix ingredients together and fill each sandwich with 3 to 4 tbs. of mixture. Add top wrapper. Coat outside of wrapper with seasoned olive oil. Cook 2 to 4 minutes.

CURRIED CHICKEN SANDWICH

Add an Indian flair to your menu with this quick and easy curry. The onions and peppers may be used raw for extra crunch. The recipe makes 4 to 6 sandwiches.

Wrapper: tortillas; white or wheat bread; pizza dough

Filling

$1/2$ cup diced onion
$1/2$ cup diced green bell pepper
$1 1/2$ tbs. vegetable oil
$1-1 1/2$ cups cooked, diced chicken
$1-1 1/2$ tbs. curry powder

Saute onion and pepper in oil 3 to 5 minutes or until golden. Off heat, add chicken and curry powder. Spread 3 to 4 tbs. filling on wrapper. Add top wrapper. Cook 2 to 4 minutes.

ENCHILADAS

Enchiladas can include many different fillings — not just the chicken, beef or beans served in many Mexican restaurants. Instead of the classic tomato sauce, you can substitute a cream sauce or even a chocolate sauce (mole). You may, of course, use an enchilada sauce bought at a grocery store.

Wrapper: tortillas; white bread

Red Tomato Sauce

1 can (10 oz.) stewed tomatoes with liquid
   (Mexican or regular)
1 medium onion
$1/2$–$3/4$ tsp. dried crushed red pepper or to taste

$1/2$ clove garlic, minced, or $1/8$ tsp. garlic powder
$1/2$ tsp. dried cilantro or $1 1/2$ tsp. fresh cilantro

Place ingredients in a blender or food processor and process until onion is finely chopped. Pour in a saucepan and cook for about 5 minutes over medium heat until sauce begins to thicken.

If desired, use 1 cup peeled, seeded, diced fresh tomatoes instead of canned, and add jalapeño peppers.

Filling

2–3 tbs. cooked, diced meat: chicken, turkey, ground meat (seasoned, if desired, with a taco
   seasoning), shrimp, crabmeat, or cooked beans
1½–2 tbs. grated Monterey Jack or cheddar cheese
salsa to taste
fresh or dried cilantro to taste
salsa, grated cheese and sour cream for garnish, optional

   Dip tortillas (or other wrapper) in sauce until wrapper is completely coated. Spread each
wrapper with 4 to 5 tbs. (3 to 4 tbs. if using bread instead of tortillas). Place top wrapper over
filling and cook 2 to 4 minutes. Garnish with salsa, cheese and sour cream, if desired.

GROUND BEEF AND SAUSAGE SANDWICH

Kids of all ages love this — keep the mixture on hand for fast and easy sandwiches.

Bread: white, whole wheat, oatmeal or sourdough

Filling

1–2 tbs. cooked, crumbled sausage (pork or turkey)
1–2 tbs. cooked, crumbled ground beef or ground turkey
1–2 slices American cheese, or 1–2 tbs. grated
salt and pepper to taste

Mix sausage and beef together and spread on bread. Layer cheese slices on top and season. Place top wrapper over filling and cook 2 to 4 minutes.

Note: If making this as a multiple recipe, simply use equal amounts of each of the 3 main ingredients — 1/2 or 1 lb. of each, seasoned to taste. It couldn't be easier!

CHILEAN EMPANADAS

This sandwich is based on a recipe normally made as a pastry turnover. You can serve this one as an appetizer or an entrée.

Wrapper: puff pastry; crescent roll dough; white, whole wheat, oatmeal or sourdough bread. If using puff pastry or crescent roll dough, add extra filling.

Filling
olive oil
2–3 tbs. cooked, crumbled ground beef or turkey
$2/3$–1 tsp. chopped onion
paprika to taste
cumin to taste
salt and pepper to taste

Coat inside of wrapper with olive oil. Mix beef and onion together and season to taste. Place top wrapper over filling and cook 2 to 4 minutes.

Note: If making a multiple recipe, use about 2 tbs. of diced onion for every $1/2$ pound of meat. Sauté both together and add seasoning.

CHICKEN EMPANADAS

Try this with leftover roasted chicken. Makes 6 to 8.

Wrapper: pizza dough; puff pastry; crescent roll dough; white or whole wheat bread. If using puff pastry or crescent roll dough, add extra filling.

Filling
1/4 cup diced green bell peppers
2 tbs. finely diced red onion
1 clove garlic, minced or 1/8 tsp. powder
olive oil, optional
2–3 tomatoes, peeled (if canned, drain) and diced
1 cup cooked, diced chicken or turkey
fresh or dried oregano, salt and pepper to taste

In a nonstick skillet, sauté peppers, onion and garlic in oil if desired. Add tomatoes, chicken and seasonings and cook until just heated. Spread 3 to 4 tbs. of mixture on wrapper. Place top wrapper over filling and cook 2 to 4 minutes.

Note: While the recipe calls for cooked chicken, you may use uncooked and sauté it with the peppers and onions.

BRAZILIAN SHRIMP EMPADINHAS

Empadinhas are Brazil's version of empanadas. Shrimp and coconut — what a combination. Canned coconut milk is available at your grocer's.

Wrapper: pizza dough; white bread; puff pastry. If using puff pastry, add extra filling.

Filling

1 lb. shrimp	2 tbs. Monterey Jack cheese
1/4 cup diced green pepper	2 egg yolks
2–3 tbs. diced onion, or to taste	1 tsp. coconut flakes
1 tsp. olive oil, optional	1/2 tsp. dried cilantro
1/2 cup coconut milk, canned	salt and pepper to taste

Sauté shrimp, green pepper and onion in a nonstick pan or with a little oil until shrimp are pink and onions are golden brown. Add remaining ingredients and boil until mixture thickens. Spread wrapper with 3 to 5 tbs. of filling. Place top wrapper over filling and cook 2 to 4 minutes.

Note: If you're using cooked shrimp, just add them in after the onion and peppers are soft. Shrimp may be easier to eat if they are diced.

MEAT STROMBOLI

Italian hams can be quite spicy, making this a great meal. Keep lots of this on hand for ready, quick sandwiches.

Wrapper: pizza dough; whole wheat, oregano, pepper, Italian, French or white bread

Outside Spread: olive oil seasoned with basil

Filling

1–2 tbs. grated provolone cheese
1–2 tbs. diced Italian ham
1–2 tbs. grated mozzarella cheese

1–2 tbs. diced Italian salami, or 1–2 slices
fresh or dried basil or oregano to taste
salt and pepper to taste

Mix meats and cheeses together and season to taste. Spread filling on wrapper. Top with second wrapper. Brush seasoned olive oil on outside of wrapper. Cook 2 to4 minutes.

Note: If making multiple sandwiches, use equal amounts of provolone, ham, mozzarella and salami.

MINTED LAMB SANDWICH

What an easy way to enjoy the great combination of lamb and mint! Ground lamb can be found in some grocery stores; if not, ask your butcher to grind some for you.

Wrapper: pita (split and cut to fit); pizza dough; whole wheat or cracked wheat bread

Outside Spread: olive oil seasoned with mint leaves

Filling:	Single	Multiple
cooked ground lamb	$1^1/_2$–2 tbs.	1 cup
cream cheese, softened	1–$1^1/_2$ tbs.	$^1/_3$ cup
dried mint leaves	$^1/_4$–$^3/_4$ tsp.	1 tbs.
garlic powder	pinch	to taste

Mix ingredients together. Spread each wrapper with 3 to 4 tbs. of mixture. Top with second wrapper. Coat outside of wrapper with seasoned olive oil. cook 2 to 4 minutes.

GREEK GYRO

Gyros are one of my all–time favorite sandwiches. This is an approximation of a gyro using ground meats. Serve with lots of the cucumber sauce!

Wrapper: pita (split and cut to fit); pizza dough; whole wheat bread

Outside Spread: olive oil seasoned with oregano, optional

Filling

1/2 lb. cooked, crumbled ground beef
1/2 lb. cooked, crumbled ground lamb
1 tsp. Italian seasoning
1 tsp. dried oregano
1 clove garlic, minced, or 1/2 tsp. garlic powder
salt and pepper to taste
1/3 cup Cucumber Yogurt Sauce

Mix all ingredients together and let sit for about 5 minutes. Spread each wrapper with 3 to 4 tbs. of mixture. Place top wrapper over filling and cook 2 to 4 minutes. Pass extra sauce.

CUCUMBER YOGURT SAUCE

1 cup plain yogurt
$\frac{1}{2}$ cup finely diced cucumber (I use the food processor)
$\frac{1}{2}$ clove garlic, minced, or $\frac{1}{4}$ tsp. garlic powder
pinch white pepper or black pepper
$\frac{1}{8}$ tsp. sugar
1 tsp. vinegar
1 tsp. olive oil

Mix ingredients together. Seasonings may be adjusted to taste. Refrigerate leftovers.

LAMB AND FETA SANDWICH

Here's another great entrée sandwich, full of robust flavor.

Wrapper: white or whole wheat bread; pizza dough; pita (split and cut to fit)

Outside Spread: olive oil seasoned with rosemary

Filling

olive oil
1½–2 tbs. cooked, crumbled ground lamb
1½–2 tbs. crumbled feta cheese
1 slice tomato
fresh or dried rosemary to taste
pinch garlic powder
salt and pepper to taste

Coat inside of wrapper with olive oil. Mix lamb and cheese together, spread over wrapper, top with tomato slice and season to taste. Top with second wrapper. Coat outside of wrapper with seasoned olive oil. Cook 2 to 4 minutes.

HAMBURGER SANDWICH

Try adding any of your favorite burger toppings right into this easy sandwich. Cooked meat may be frozen in small portions for fast thawing and serving.

Bread: whole wheat, cracked wheat, multi–grain, white or oatmeal

Filling

ketchup, mayonnaise, mustard, or salad dressing, your choice
2–3 tbs. cooked, crumbled ground beef or turkey
1–2 slices cheddar cheese, or 1–2 tbs. grated, optional
1–2 tbs. cooked bacon, crumbled, optional
1–2 tsp. blue cheese, crumbled, optional
$1/2$–1 tsp. finely diced onions, optional
1–2 mushrooms, thinly sliced, optional
1–$1 1/2$ tbs. crushed pineapple, drained, optional
1–2 pickle slices, optional

Spread condiment of choice on inside of bread. Top with ground meat and your choice of remaining ingredients. Place top wrapper over filling and cook 2 to 4 minutes.

BOREK

This is based on a Turkish recipe, adapted for the sandwich maker. Normally boreks use a puff pastry or phyllo casing and are baked or fried.

Wrapper: puff pastry; pita (split and cut to fit), whole wheat or cracked wheat bread; phyllo. If using puff pastry or phyllo, add extra filling.

Filling
1–1½ tsp. olive oil
¾ tsp. red wine vinegar
2–3 tbs. cooked, crumbled ground beef
¾–1 tsp. pine nuts
½–1 tsp. chopped onion
ground allspice to taste
fresh or dried dill to taste
salt and pepper to taste

Combine olive oil and vinegar; coat inside of wrapper. Mix ground beef, pine nuts, onion and seasonings. Spread wrapper with filling. Place top wrapper over filling and cook 2 to 4 minutes.

BARBECUED PORK SANDWICH

If you live in the South, you are sure to have access to great barbecued pork. If you want to make your own, here is a very quick and easy recipe.

Bread: whole wheat, oatmeal, white or sourdough

Filling

1 lb. country style ribs

2/3 cup barbecue sauce, or more to taste

Marinate ribs in sauce, refrigerated, for about 4 hours. Bring up to room temperature while you preheat oven to 350°. Roast in a covered pan for 1 to 1½ hours, basting frequently. Shred roasted pork; add more barbecue sauce if necessary. Top a slice of bread with about 3 to 4 tbs. of meat. Place top wrapper over filling and cook 2 to 4 minutes.

As an alternative, serve with coleslaw on the side or cook it in the sandwich.

EGG ROLL

This is a dieter's delight. Experiment with different vegetables: mushrooms, baby corn, celery, bok choy. A pinch of ground ginger may be used in place of the fresh ginger; you can also serve filling over rice. Makes about 16 to 20 egg rolls or 32 to 40 appetizers.

Wrapper: egg roll wrapper; tortillas (I much prefer tortillas); white bread

Filling

1/4 cup grated carrot

1/4 cup diced green peppers

1/4 cup diced green beans

1/4 cup diced cabbage

1/4 cup diced water chestnuts

1/2 cup bean sprouts

1 1/3 tbs. sesame oil

1/2 cup diced cooked beef, chicken, turkey or shrimp

1 tsp. minced fresh ginger

1/4 tsp. mustard powder

1 clove garlic, minced, or 1/4 tsp. garlic powder

2–3 tbs. soy sauce

Stir–fry or sauté all ingredients in a wok or frying pan. Vegetables should remain crisp. Spread each wrapper with 3 to 4 tbs. of mixture. Place top wrapper over filling and cook 2 to 4 minutes.

LUMPIA

Similar to the egg roll, this dish is from the Philippines. Makes 16 to 20 lumpia or 32 to 40 appetizers.

Wrapper: egg roll wrappers; tortillas (I much prefer tortillas); white bread

Filling

$1/2$ cup cooked, crumbled ground pork
$1/2$ cup cooked, crumbled ground beef
$1/2$ cup diced shrimp
2 tsp. diced onions
3 tbs. diced mushrooms
3 tbs. grated carrot

$1 1/2$ tbs. diced green onion
$3/4$ cup shredded wong bok or cabbage
3 tbs. soy sauce
minced garlic or garlic powder to taste
salt and pepper to taste

Stir–fry all ingredients in a wok or frying pan. Vegetables should remain crisp. If shrimp are not precooked, stir–fry first until they will turn pink, and then add vegetables. Spread each wrapper with 3 to 4 tbs. of filling. Place top wrapper over filling and cook 2 to 4 minutes.

GARLIC BREAD GALORE

Who can resist a good garlic bread? It's the perfect accompaniment to a favorite Italian meal.

Bread: thick-sliced Italian, white or French

Spread
1–2 tbs. melted butter
1 clove garlic, minced, or 1/8–1/4 tsp. garlic powder
1 tsp. dried parsley or 1 tbs. fresh chopped parsley

Combine ingredients and spread on both sides of each slice of bread. Heat the bread in the sandwich maker 2 to 3 minutes. If desired, you can fill the sandwich with spaghetti sauce.

DESSERTS IN MINUTES

In addition to the dessert ideas I present here, don't overlook some extremely quick and easy desserts found in your grocery aisle. Try canned pie fillings in unbaked pie crusts — remember to use enough filling and bake for about 4 to 5 minutes. Do not latch the machine closed. Cake mixes bake quite well in the sandwich maker. Spoon enough batter into each scalloped section so that it is full but not overflowing. Keep an eye on the baking process, checking it every minute or so with a toothpick. It's a fine line between fully baked and starting to burn. Who can beat fresh cake in about 5 minutes!

APPLE PIE

Apple pie is everyone's favorite. Here's a quick way to get a piece of pie without lots of bother.

Wrapper: unbaked pie crust; puff pastry; raisin or nut bread. If using unbaked pie crust or puff pastry, add extra apple slices to make a nice, full pie.

Filling

1–1½ tbs. heavy cream	1–1½ tsp. sugar
1½–2 tsp. flour	pinch salt
pinch cinnamon	thin apple slices, about ¼ apple

Mix together cream, flour, cinnamon, sugar and salt. Spread apples on wrapper and pour cream mixture over apples. Place top wrapper over filling and cook 4 to 5 minutes, unlatching machine after 1 minute.

Note: If preparing apples ahead of time, sprinkle apple slices with ½ to 1 tsp. orange or lemon juice to prevent discoloration. For variety, substitute mangos, peaches or papaya for apples.

PEACH TURNOVER

Cream cheese and peaches make a decadent dessert.

Wrapper: white, Italian or French bread; unbaked pie crust; puff pastry; raisin or nut bread. If using pie crust or puff pastry, add more peach slices..

Filling
1–1½ tbs. cream cheese, softened
1–1½ tbs. confectioners' sugar
dash vanilla extract
pinch cinnamon
thin peach slices, about ¼–½ peach

Mix cream cheese, sugar, vanilla and cinnamon together until well blended. Spread inside wrapper and layer peaches on top. Place top wrapper over filling and cook 4 to 5 minutes, unlatching machine after 1 minute.

CHERRY TURNOVER

Wrapper: Italian or French bread; unbaked pie crust; puff pastry; raisin bread.

Filling

2–3 tbs. cream cheese

1/4–1/3 tsp. sugar

3–4 maraschino cherries, chopped

1–1 1/2 tsp. chopped macadamia nuts or
    walnuts

Mix ingredients together until well blended and spread filling on wrapper. Place top wrapper over filling and cook 4 to 5 minutes, unlatching machine after 1 minute.

CRANBERRY ORANGE TURNOVER

Wrapper: Italian or French bread; unbaked pie crust; puff pastry; raisin or nut bread.

Filling

1–1 1/2 tbs. cream cheese

2–2 1/2 tbs. cranberry sauce

1/3–1/2 tsp. confectioners' sugar

3–6 mandarin orange segments

1/3–1/2 tsp. dried mint leaves

Mix ingredients together until well blended and fill turnover. Place top wrapper over filling and cook 4 to 5 minutes, unlatching machine after 1 minute.

PUMPKIN CHEESE NUT TURNOVER

Make and freeze your own pumpkin puree or keep canned pumpkin on hand to enjoy this year-round.

Wrapper: puff pastry; nut or raisin bread; pumpkin bread. If using puff pastry, add extra filling.

Filling

1¼ tsp. pumpkin puree or canned pumpkin
1–1¼ tbs. softened cream cheese
1–1¼ tbs. confectioners' sugar

pinch pumpkin pie spice
1–1¼ tsp. chopped nuts

Mix ingredients together until well blended and spread on wrapper. Place top wrapper over filling and cook 4 to 5 minutes, unlatching machine after 1 minute.

HOLIDAY TREATS

Easy–to–make–and–serve sweet appetizers or desserts, these will disappear quickly.

Wrapper: quick breads such as pumpkin, carrot, zucchini, strawberry or orange

Filling

4 oz. ($\frac{1}{2}$ cup) cream cheese, softened

$\frac{1}{2}$ cup confectioners' sugar

$\frac{1}{4}$ tsp. vanilla extract

$\frac{1}{2}$ cup chopped walnuts or pecans

Mix ingredients together until well blended and spread wrapper with $1\frac{1}{2}$ to $2\frac{1}{2}$ tbs. of mixture. Top with second wrapper and cook 2 to 4 minutes.

CHOCOLATE BANANA DESSERT

Truly an easy, throw–together dessert that everyone will enjoy.

Wrapper: nut, banana or white bread; pizza dough

Filling

1–$1\frac{1}{2}$ tbs. mashed banana

$\frac{3}{4}$–1 tsp. chopped walnuts or macadamia nuts

$1\frac{1}{2}$–2 tsp. Nutella (chocolate–hazelnut spread)

Mix ingredients together until well blended and spread wrapper with filling. Top with second wrapper and bake 2 to 4 minutes.

BANANA PIE

Here's a fabulous use for the overripe banana when you don't have enough for banana bread.

Wrapper: puff pastry; crescent roll dough; white, nut, raisin or banana bread. If using puff pastry or crescent roll dough, add extra filling.

Filling
1½–2 tbs. mashed banana
2 tsp.–1 tbs. cream cheese, softened
2 tsp.– 1 tbs. confectioners' sugar
dash vanilla extract
1–1½ tsp. chopped walnuts or macadamia nuts
confectioners' sugar for garnish, optional

Mix ingredients together and spread wrapper with filling. Top with second wrapper and cook 2 to 4 minutes.

CHOCOLATE NUT DELIGHT

Wrapper: white or nut bread

Filling

2–2½ tbs. Nutella (chocolate-hazelnut spread)   1–1½ tbs. chopped almonds or walnuts
1–1½ tbs. marshmallow cream

Mix ingredients together until well blended and spread wrapper with filling. Top with second wrapper and cook 2 to 4 minutes.

HAWAIIAN DELIGHT

Wrapper: unbaked pie crust; crescent roll dough; puff pastry; white bread. If using crescent roll dough or puff pastry, add extra filling.

Filling

2–2½ tbs. Nutella (chocolate-hazelnut spread)   1–1¼ tbs. coconut flakes
1½–2 tbs. coconut milk   1–1½ tbs. chopped macadamia nuts
⅔ –1 tsp. confectioners' sugar

Mix ingredients together until well blended and spread wrapper with filling. Top with second wrapper and cook 2 to 4 minutes.

CARROT CAKE

This is an absolutely wonderful carrot cake with a crunchy crust. Great for those evenings when the sweet tooth hits but you don't want to bake a whole cake! Makes 2 to 3 servings.

1/2 cup grated carrot
1/4 cup vegetable oil
1 egg
1/2 cup sugar
1/2 tsp. cinnamon
1/2 tsp. baking soda
1/2 cup self–rising flour
1/4 cup oats, regular or quick
2 tbs. chopped walnuts, optional

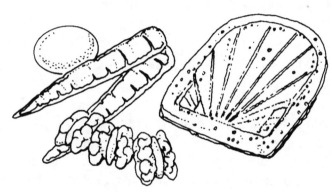

Beat together carrot, oil and egg. Add sugar, cinnamon, baking soda, flour and oats; mix well. Add walnuts if desired. Spoon batter into scallops until full but not overflowing. Bake for about 5 to 7 minutes, unlatching the machine after 1 minute and checking often for doneness.

PUMPKIN OATMEAL CAKE

You can't beat this for ease and quickness when you want something sweet. Great in the fall if using fresh, cooked pumpkin. Makes 2 or 3 servings.

$^1/_2$ cup canned or cooked, pureed pumpkin
2 tbs. vegetable oil
1 egg
$^1/_3$ cup brown sugar, firmly packed
$^3/_4$ tsp. pumpkin pie spice
$^1/_2$ cup biscuit mix
$^1/_3$ cup oats, regular or quick
2–3 tbs. chopped walnuts or pecans, optional

Beat together pumpkin, oil and egg. Add brown sugar, pumpkin pie spice, biscuit mix and oats; mix well. Add nuts if desired. Spoon batter into scallops until full but not over-flowing. Bake for about 4 to 5 minutes, unlatching the machine after 1 minute and checking often for doneness.

APPLE SPICE PIE

This treat is a delightful cross between an apple pie and spice cake.

Wrapper: unbaked pie crust; puff pastry; white bread. If using puff pastry, add extra filling.

Filling
1½–2 tbs. applesauce
pumpkin pie spice to taste
½–¾ tsp. brown sugar, firmly packed
2 tsp.–1 tbs. all-purpose flour
1–1½ tbs. chopped walnuts, optional
1–1½ tbs. raisins, optional

Season applesauce with pumpkin pie spice to taste. Add sugar, flour, walnuts and raisins if desired. Spread filling on wrapper. Top with second wrapper. Bake for about 3 to 4 minutes.

SUGARED PUMPKIN GOODIES

These pumpkin treats are sure to make a hit during the fall and holiday season. Try substituting Craisins (sweetened, dried cranberries) for the raisins in this recipe.

Wrapper: unbaked pie crust; crescent roll or biscuit dough; puff pastry; white bread. Use extra filling unless using white bread.

Filling
2–3 tbs. canned or cooked, pureed pumpkin
1–1½ tbs. brown sugar
1–1½ tbs. chopped walnuts
2–3 tsp. raisins
pinch pumpkin pie spice

Mix ingredients together and spread wrapper with filling. Top with second wrapper and bake 2 to 4 minutes.

NUT TREAT

Wrapper: cinnamon raisin bread; puff pastry; crescent roll dough. Adjust filling to wrapper.

Filling

2–3 tbs. finely chopped walnuts

2 tsp.–1 tbs. finely chopped almonds

1–2 tsp. confectioners' sugar

1–1⅓ tbs. cream cheese

Mix all ingredients together; spread wrapper with filling. Top with second wrapper and bake 2 to 4 minutes.

AMARETTO CHOCOLATE TRIANGLES

Wrapper: crescent roll dough; puff pastry; unbaked pie crust; white bread. Adjust filling to wrapper.

Filling

2–3 tbs. Nutella (chocolate–hazelnut spread)

2–2½ tsp. Amaretto liqueur

1–1½ tbs. finely chopped almonds

2–3 tsp. confectioners' sugar

Mix all ingredients together; spread wrapper with filling. Top with second wrapper and bake 2 to 4 minutes.

INDEX

Serve Creative, Easy, Nutritious Meals with nitty gritty® Cookbooks

100 Dynamite Desserts
The 9 x 13 Pan Cookbook
The Barbecue Cookbook
Beer and Good Food
The Best Bagels are Made at Home
The Best Pizza is Made at Home
The Big Book of Bread Machine Recipes
Blender Drinks
Bread Baking
Bread Machine Cookbook
Bread Machine Cookbook II
Bread Machine Cookbook III
Bread Machine Cookbook V
Bread Machine Cookbook VI
The Little Burger Bible
Cappuccino/Espresso
Casseroles
The Coffee Book
Convection Oven Cookery
The Cook-Ahead Cookbook
Cooking for 1 or 2
Cooking in Clay

Cooking in Porcelain
Cooking on the Indoor Grill
Cooking with Chile Peppers
Cooking with Grains
Cooking with Your Kids
New Recipes for your Deep Fryer
The Dehydrator Cookbook
Edible Pockets for Every Meal
Entrées from Your Bread Machine
Extra-Special Crockery Pot Recipes
Fabulous Fiber Cookery
Fondue and Hot Dips
Fresh Vegetables
From Freezer, 'Fridge and Pantry
From Your Ice Cream Maker
The Garlic Cookbook
Healthy Cooking on the Run
Healthy Snacks for Kids
The Juicer Book
The Juicer Book II
Lowfat American Favorites
New International Fondue Cookbook

No Salt, No Sugar, No Fat
One-Dish Meals
The Pasta Machine Cookbook
Pinch of Time: Meals in Less than 30
    Minutes
Quick and Easy Pasta Recipes
Recipes for the Loaf Pan
Recipes for the Pressure Cooker
Risottos, Paellas, and other Rice
    Specialties
Rotisserie Oven Cooking
New Recipes for Your Sandwich Maker
The Sensational Skillet: Sautés and Stir-Fries
Slow Cooking in Crock-Pot,® Slow Cooker,
    Oven and Multi-Cooker
Soups and Stews
Tapas Fantasticas
The Toaster Oven Cookbook
Unbeatable Chicken Recipes
The Vegetarian Slow Cooker
New Waffles and Pizzelles
Wraps and Roll-Ups

For a free catalog, call: Bristol Publishing Enterprises.
(800) 346-4889
www.bristolpublishing.com